E400

Native American
WOMEN

Native American
WOMEN

 DIANA STEER

BARNES
&NOBLE
BOOKS
NEW YORK

FOREWORD

In 1920 American women won a hard-fought battle with the inclusion of the Nineteenth Amendment into the American Constitution. Yet this victory largely impacted on fulfilling the citizenship rights of *white* women. What had always been the birthright of native women was just beginning to be experienced by their white sisters. Native women, who had always been considered the backbone of their respective nations, had been disenfranchised and made powerless by the European conquerors.

Unfortunately, there have been entirely too few systematic studies of the true role of native women in their traditional societies. History has either misinterpreted, misrepresented or failed to address accurately the importance of native women. Cherokee author Rayna Green has described America's portrayal of native women as "the Pocahontas Perplex."

But such cultural and gender bias can be corrected by providing a richer understanding of native cultures and the position of native women within them. Their voices need to be heard and their histories need to be told. American society has been rather tenacious in holding on to its stereotypical image of "Indians"; a misconception which has been told, retold and believed for generations. Yet the persistence of native people has enabled them to survive the cultural assault inflicted on their traditions and values.

Native American Women offers the reader, in an informative and instructive manner, a glimpse of the true nature of native women through stories and photographs. This is the strategy for fighting and destroying myths.

Trudie Lamb Richmond,
Institute for American Indian Studies,
Schaghticoke Reservation, Connecticut

Library of Congress Cataloging in Publication Data available

ISBN: 0-7607-0006-0

Printed in China

10 9 8 7 6 5 4 3 2 1

Diana Steer, novelist and nonfiction author, combines her writing career with economic development research on reservations.

CONTENTS

INTRODUCTION

Western civilization's patriarchal society tends to ignore the unique perspective that women bring to the issues facing them. Partly as a result of this inherent bias, the central roles native women played in their aboriginal cultures was radically misunderstood by the Europeans who came to take their lands.

This book is a general introduction to the central and critically important roles of Native American women. Within the constraints imposed by space, not only are common themes throughout the five hundred indigenous nations addressed, but also specific aspects of the lives of women as they played, raised families, and worked in the Lakota, Cherokee, Iroquois, Apache, Navajo, Cree, Inuit and other nations. While references are made to the native nations living within what are now called Central and South America, this book focuses on North America during the evolution from traditional lifestyles to the present.

The research for this book came from a number of sources, including the knowledge I have been given by native people I have come to know and love, and many books they recommended. Through more formal interviews I had the honor of meeting new people kind enough to share their thoughts.

In a classically constructed book, the material is logically divided into sections and chapters. But an intensely holistic subject like native life won't divide so easily. In native life, all endeavors, from the making of a simple utensil to the creation of highly complex decorations, are seen as outlets for the individual soul. Indigenous people see all of life as holy, the sacred and the mundane as one.

Not long ago, Native Americans were casually dismissed as members of a "vanishing race." In the space of a few hundred years, westerners have managed to take the thin envelope in which we live on Mother Earth to the brink of destruction, perhaps endangering all cultures. Women-centered societies are descended from cultures that managed to live in harmony with nature for a million generations.

With gratitude for keeping the sacred fire burning through dark nights, this book is dedicated to "the mothers of the Nations."

DIANA STEER
CONNECTICUT, 1996

MOTHERS OF THE NATIONS

A nation is not conquered until the hearts of its women are on the ground.
  —TRADITIONAL CHEYENNE SAYING

The council-tent is our Congress, and anybody can speak who has any-thing to say, women and all…If women could go into your Congress, I think justice would soon be done to the Indians.
  —SARAH WINNEMUCCA, PAIUTE ACTIVIST, 1883

THE CENTRALITY OF NATIVE WOMEN

To begin to understand the native cultures of North America and why they were so successful in living with nature, one must first comprehend the central role played by native women and the deep respect accorded them by their societies. Women were critically important and recognized as the life-bearers and nurturers of the nation. While their role differed from that of the men, they were not seen as inferior. The wise women of most nations were consulted with the same respect accorded men.

In matrifocal communities, society is not ruled by women in the way that patriarchal societies today are ruled by men—with heavy emphasis on hierarchy, obedience to authority and a tendency toward vastly unequal distributions of wealth and power. Matrifocal societies tend to be communal, life-centered and strongly concerned with the needs of all of the people. The woman's role was to care for her children, and the reason for a man's very existence was to support her in this by providing meat and protection against enemies. In an egalitarian system, everyone, regardless of sex and age, has a place in the life of the nation.

In the white male-dominated culture of the United States today, it can be difficult at first to grasp just how radically different life under a truly matrifocal society can be for *all* of its citizens—women, children and men as well. Everyone benefits in a culture that is based upon protecting, nurturing and respecting all of life.

For the most part, women contributed to the nation's well-being through the care with which they raised their children and looked after their families. However, beyond the childbearing years, their roles took on wider dimensions, expanding into politics and also into the spiritual realm, where many became medicine or holy people. The men took care of the tribe mainly through their skills in hunting and, when necessary, in war.

Opposite: *Mother and child at the Jémez Pueblo, circa 1912. Indigenous women are proud to be women, proud to be mothers. They are accorded deep respect for their critical role of bearing and raising the next generation.*

9

Below: Ute woman and children, circa 1900. In native cultures, children are treated with love and kindness; harsh treatment is almost unknown. The traditional object of child rearing was to produce adults who had both a strong sense of responsibility for the community and self-respect.

In tribal life, both female and male children were raised to be strong and to think for themselves. On the other hand, they also knew that, ultimately, their personal importance lay in the support, care and in extreme cases the personal self-sacrifice that they could offer to further the welfare of their nation. By the same token, those living a tribal life knew that, should they find themselves in any kind of trouble or danger, the others in turn would take care of them. Among first people the world over, hospitality is a virtue with few equals. A hungry person is never turned from the door. Among the Plains people, a man who wished to show his prowess and gain honors would offer part of his kill after a hunt to the widows and old people who could not provide for themselves.

As opposed to the competitive individualistic western values of today, the strong and talented among native people demonstrated their superior abilities not by shunting aside the weak, but by taking care of them. One of the requirements of a chief was that he allow no one in his band to go hungry—if necessary, he must feed them himself. He led by example, not coercion. Among the Iroquois, it was the women who chose the chiefs (who were always men) and could remove them if they proved themselves unworthy.

This virtue of sacrifice for others, which could be seen as "female" in western eyes, survives among native women and men today, where great respect is accorded that person of whom it may be said that she or he "works for The People."

SIMILARITIES AMONG THE WOMEN OF NATIVE NATIONS

When one looks at the ways in which Indian women lived their lives within the vast array of native nations, it is striking to observe the similarities, despite the fact that there were at least 350 distinct nations in the area that is now the mainland United States, 500 nations if Canada is included. Indian women of these nations had in almost all respects far more in common with each other than they did with any of the European women whose culture came to dominate their land.

A deep reverence for Mother Earth is basic to all Indian nations, and this reverence for life is reflected in the respect that they accord to women as the bearers and nurturers of that life. Operating under such belief systems, these societies were prone to rape neither women nor the Earth itself, a lesson for today's civilization which is prone to violence against both Earth and women.

Below: Travois of Fasting Woman of the Blackfoot Nation, photographed by Walter McClintock. For the highly mobile Plains Indians, women's domestic skills included the ability to strike camp quickly, load belongings onto the travois and set up again in the new location—rarely with the assistance of men.

Matrilocal organization of societies was to be found across most of the continent, in which men go to reside with the families of their wives and, in the case of a divorce, it is her family who will help her raise the children. Both her male and female children become members of her clan and nation.

While firm division of labor between the sexes is typical and strongly adhered to, there seems an equal tolerance and respect for those few individuals who feel drawn to doing the work of the other sex. While most women could take up arms of a sort in response to an emergency, for example if the camp were attacked while the men were away, a few "manly hearted" women knew from childhood that the life of the warrior was to become their own, and they were allowed to be true to their path, some never marrying.

Among Plains tribes, there were several celebrated women warriors. A few women even led men into battle. Minnie Hollow Wood, a Lakota, won the right to wear a war bonnet, a rare honor for a woman, for her participation in fights with the U.S. cavalry. Many women accompanied brothers and husbands when these men went to war and distinguished themselves with skill and daring, helping rescue a hero surrounded by his enemies or dashing into the thick of the fight to retrieve a fallen one. As a teenager, Elk Hollering in the Water of the Blackfeet Sioux won honors by accompanying her husband on raids against enemy tribes.

After citizenship was granted to Native Americans in 1924, native women were to serve in all subsequent foreign wars in which the United States engaged, as did their men. In fact, by percentage, native people have given more of their children to the armed services of the United States than any other minority group. Since World War II, 70 percent of eligible Native Americans have served in the armed forces, compared to approximately 15 percent of the eligible white population. Today, Indians are three times as likely to serve as non-Indians.

While women could become warriors if strongly motivated to do so, by the same token, men who were drawn to doing women's work, to living as women, were understood to be different from the hunter-warrior class of men and accepted as such. *Winktes*, as they were called among the Lakota, dressed in women's clothes, stayed in camp to work alongside the women when the men went out to hunt and were considered to possess unique spiritual powers.

A comparative lack of racism as we know it today was also a common element among many Indian nations. This may be seen in their adoption of Europeans into their nations when whites first came to this shore. The European conquerors brought with them

Left: *The Anadarko Oklahoma Annual All American Inter-tribal Exposition is held in August. A young woman is chosen to lead the powwow. In this photograph the leader opens the powwow with sign language. Held across North America in the warm summer months, powwows feature dance competitions and art and craft displays.*

an extreme obsession with race, based upon the need to establish moral and economic superiority over the subjugated. This gave them, in effect, the "right" to take what was not theirs.

In the great Indian wars when whites pushed across native lands, it was common practice for Indians to take whites as captives for the purpose of replacing the labor provided by Indian dead. This was considered helpful for families who had lost a hunter critical to the food supply, a mother needed to care for children or children for the bereft. Mary Jemison is but one example of a white child taken into an Indian family who had lost a loved one. Having lost her own family of origin at the hands of Indian warriors from another nation, Mary learned to live as a Seneca among her new sisters. She remained with her new people for the rest of her life, marrying and bearing children.

Above: Native women worked together on many projects, including the creation of tipi covers. This photograph by Walter McClintock shows some of the designs used to decorate tipis. Traditionally, an older woman skilled in the craft supervised the construction of the cover, a large undertaking that could use several buffalo skins.

Whites captured in battle were brought to camp, where the women heads of clans decided whether the captive was killed or was saved and adopted by a selected family. This forms part of the background of the famous Pocahontas story. The young girl, while not in love with the much older John Smith, had decided that he should be saved for adoption.

Paula Gunn Allen is a professor of English at the University of California, Los Angeles, and an American Indian of Laguna Pueblo and Lakota heritage. She is the author of several books and writes incisively on the topic of Indian people in general and Indian women in particular. Of the commonality to be found amongst native peoples, she says, "…while the distinctions among native communities are many and, linguistically at least, the differences are vast, the similarities are far greater and much more profound.

"I have believed for some time that the similarities in world view and spiritual understanding are marked because the supernaturals who live on this continent with us possess marked similarities among themselves, and so their teachings to us are similar, varying because of locale and because of the language and histories of the various peoples they instruct. Perhaps differences exist because different landscapes give rise to different spirits or supernaturals."

Left: Navajo sand paintings are an essential aspect of the sacred healing arts. In a healing ceremony, or Chant way, a healer trickles finely powdered colored sandstone onto a bed of fresh sand. The patient sits on the painting facing east, the direction from which all Navajo blessings come. After the Chant way, the healer ceremonially disposes of the sand, said to have captured the source of the patient's disharmony.

CENTRALITY OF WOMEN IN TRIBAL ORIGINATION STORIES

Woman is forever, eternal. Man comes from woman and to woman he returns.

—OJIBWA SAYING

The centrality of women and the respect accorded the female among Indian nations is demonstrated in the tribal origination stories, where it is the woman who is first formed, and it is from

Left: Today, Taos Pueblo looks much like it did when it was built 2,000 years ago. It stands at the base of 13,000-foot Wheeler Peak in New Mexico. Inhabitants live as their ancestors did, speaking the ancient Tewa language and drawing water from a stream that descends from the sacred Blue Lake. The pueblo has no electricity, and all baking is done in large outdoor ovens.

her that man springs. This is quite the opposite of the Christian origination legend of Adam and Eve, where Adam was not only the first created, but Eve was seen as a sinful, fearsome creature, who deceived man with that foolish business of the apple. By contrast, in the native world, woman is seen as wise, powerful and good. A Keres ceremonial prayer begins, "She is the mother of all, in fertility, in holding, in taking us again back to her breast." As stated by a Lakota elder, "It is well to be good to women in the strength of our manhood, because we must sit under their hands at both ends of our lives."

In many origination stories, it is most often a female power or goddess, not a male god, who creates life and even the Earth herself through the power of the Great Spirit. The Great Spirit, also called the Great Mystery, is the generative force of the universe, the magic behind all powers. Among the Iroquois, the female goddess of creation is appropriately named Sky Woman, who came down from the sky to bring life to Earth. Among the Inuit, Sedna brings the fish and other game of the sea. Among the Shawnee of Oklahoma, a holy woman named Our Grandmother created humankind. She also gave the Shawnee their code of ethics and most of their religious ceremonies. She lives now in a celestial bark house and, because the Shawnee believe she likes to see her grandchildren dance, they continue to perform the songs and dances she taught them long ago.

Ancient flood stories dot the landscape of aboriginal legends, reminiscent of Noah's ark. The Shawnee's holy woman, Our

Below: An extended family of Lakota in Wyoming, probably in the late 1890s. At the center, a man of the family sits with a long-stemmed calumet pipe, a copy of the ancient sacred pipe brought to the Lakota by the legendary White Buffalo Calf Woman. When not in use, the stem and bowl were wrapped separately and stored in a bag.

Grandmother, recreated humankind after being the only survivor of a great flood.

Born of darkness and dawn, Changing Woman of the Navajo and Apache was imbued with the generative power of the female at her puberty ceremony, which is still practiced by the people today when their own daughters come of age. Changing Woman created the corn plant and later, with pieces of her own flesh, she created the First People, the ancestors of the Navajo. She also gave the tribe the highly sacred Blessingway ceremony, sung for healing purposes. The Lakota were also given their ceremonies by a holy woman.

White Buffalo Calf Woman appeared to the Lakota on the Great Plains as a beautiful maiden dressed in white buckskin. She came carrying the first ancient sacred pipe—still in existence and kept in a secret place by medicine man Chief Arvol Looking Horse. White Buffalo Calf Woman explained to The People that the pipe bowl represented the earth and that the wooden stem which was fitted into the bowl when smoking was to commence represented all growing things. The bowl and stem might also be seen as the male and female powers that, when joined together, form the very unity of creation. Whoever prayed with a sacred pipe such as this would be in harmony with the universe, hence the famous "peace pipe." Sacred pipes that are made today are designed along the same lines as the original. Their bowls are often carved of blood stone and the stems are sturdy ash decorated with feathers, beads and other items of sacred significance to the owner.

Not speaking truthfully while smoking a sacred pipe is inconceivable to Indians, which was why the pipe-smoking ceremony was always requested when they attempted to make treaties with white government officials. Unfortunately, the government officials were reluctant to comprehend this fine point and, to date, every treaty that the United States signed with Indian nations has been broken.

While she stayed among the Lakota People, White Buffalo Calf Woman disclosed many mysteries and ceremonials, and then, transforming herself into a white buffalo calf, she disappeared, leaving her sacred pipe and her spiritual teachings with The People.

Today, the Lakota People feel that a major spiritual turning point in the life of indigenous people and of the Earth has been reached. On August 20, 1993, a white buffalo calf was born on a ranch in Wisconsin, the first such known birth in one hundred years. The last white buffalo known to exist died in 1959. The birth is a notable occurrence by any standard given the fact that white buffalo were extremely rare even during the days of the great herds, when millions roamed the plains. According to the American Bison Association, the odds of a white buffalo being born are about one in ten million. Considering the few survivors left to roam the fenced-in plains of today, the little calf is a miracle indeed, and so is aptly named "Miracle."

Native people have observed that, while Mother Earth gives forth life, she is impregnated by the rays of Father Sun. The first Zuni People to settle in the Southwest had to depend upon a modest diet of grasses until Father Sun sent them the Six Corn Maidens, beautiful sisters who danced among the grasses and transformed them into life-giving corn of many colors: yellow, blue, red, white, speckled and black. Today many Pueblo villages choose young women to represent the Corn Maidens at festivals to bless the harvest.

Corn, developed by Indians in the Americas and considered one of the world's food treasures, gained among native peoples a religious significance. It served as a holy offering, a medium for the anointing of priests, an integral part of every important celebration. The Navajo greet the dawn with a sprinkling of corn. The Iroquois

Below: Hopi women cleaning corn. Photograph by Charles Carpenter, 1901.

Above: Apache woman working in a field, turn of the century.

honor the Three Sisters for bringing them not only corn, but beans and squash as well. Among the Cherokee, Selu is the corn giver. Her name in Cherokee means maize. The first woman, she nourished her children with corn and beans from her very body. Rubbing her stomach, she produced ears of corn from between her legs. From her breasts came green beans. She was mistakenly killed as a sorceress, but before she died Selu instructed her sons to drag her corpse through the clearing in the woods seven times to ensure an abundant and endless supply of grain for her descendants. The lazy boys did a poor job and as a consequence, corn grows only in scattered areas of the Cherokee's native Appalachia and requires cultivation. Selu lives on at the end of the world, watching over her people.

WHITE INVASION AND ITS AFTERMATH

Where are your women?

—OUTACITTY, CHEROKEE LEADER, UPON MEETING WITH
BRITISH REPRESENTATIVES, EARLY EIGHTEENTH CENTURY

The first European men to come to the New World did not bring their women and families with them. At least part of this may be attributed to concern for danger in an unknown land. The Indians, upon observing the strange phenomenon of men without women, decided that the violent and often crazy behavior exhibited by whites stemmed in part from this fact.

When white men first saw native women, they observed that, compared to the women back home, natives had greater sexual freedom and much more hard physical labor to perform in the fields. But the men did not understand what they observed. Native women were considered mistresses of their own bodies, could choose their own husbands and divorce them at will. In eighteenth-century European male eyes, this was viewed as sexual promiscuity. Europeans either did not know about or did not wish to understand the sexual restraint exercised by couples who practiced birth control, limiting the number of children for the welfare of mother, child and, during lean periods, of tribe as well. Observing Indian women at work in the fields, European men did not know or did not care to know that those fields and their harvest were owned by the women and that an outdoor life of hard work, punctuated by a great deal of leisure time, was a far more healthy lifestyle than that of native women's European counterparts.

While some more enlightened souls understood and appreciated the role that native women played in their nations, the majority of European men simply wrote native women off as wantons or drudges. Not wishing to discover that native women might be

Right: Early photograph of women on a reservation. During the 1800s, when the U.S. government forced native nations onto reservations, the traditional power of native women began to wane. Native men could no longer hunt to feed their families, and white agents worked hard to turn them into farmers. Agriculture, once the realm of women, was thus taken from them.

Above: In this painting by Mary Diven Wright, men and women of the Arapaho Nation dance the Ghost Dance.

living a more rewarding life, European women were in the main not at pains to contradict this view.

During the terrible wars of the eighteenth and nineteenth centuries, which devastated Indian nations across the continent, whites laid waste to the women's carefully tended fields of corn and fruit trees. As the Americans conquered Indian lands to the west, so too did they attempt to conquer the Indians themselves. They did so by demanding that Indians become like whites: patriarchal, secular and individualistic. Through the efforts of government agents and missionaries, Indians were Europeanized. This broke up their strong clan systems into individualized, less powerful, nuclear families, headed by men who, it was thought, could be more easily controlled by the U.S. Government. This led to general demoralization of the population and the attendant problems of depression, alcoholism and suicide still faced by Indian nations today.

In the late nineteenth century, in a desperate attempt to bring back the old ways, a new religion was started by a Paiute named Wovoka. Wovoka preached that if all Indian people prayed and danced, the dead would arise, the buffalo would return and the white man would leave forever. This Ghost Dance religion swept like wildfire across the western Indian nations, who were desperate with grief over the loss of their people, of their ancient and bal-

Above: Native camp near Fort Laramie, Wyoming, 1868. This could have been the village in which the famous chief Red Cloud stayed during the signing of the Fort Laramie Treaty of 1868. The treaty delineated the boundaries of what came to be called the Great Sioux Reservation. It was barely signed before it was broken by gold-seeking whites illegally trespassing in the sacred Black Hills.

anced way of life. It is hard to imagine what it must have been like to live in a world where half the people you had known and loved since childhood were either in prison or dead.

The Ghost Dance movement terrified white settlers, who assumed that it was designed to whip Indians into a white-killing frenzy. The tragic massacre at Wounded Knee Creek, South Dakota, in December of 1890 was in part a reaction to the new Ghost Dance religion, which had taken strong hold among the Lakota. There, three hundred unarmed Minneconjou women, children and men were gunned down by remnants of the late Colonel Custer's former regiment. The Indian leader, Chief Big Foot, was seriously ill with pneumonia at the time, and he had surrendered to the troops, who he had assumed would lead his people to Pine Ridge, where other Lakota Indians were living. It was the fourth day after Christmas that the first torn and bleeding bodies were carried into the Episcopal Church at Pine Ridge. Across the chancel front above the pulpit was strung the banner: PEACE ON EARTH, GOOD WILL TO MEN. This massacre, formerly termed a "battle" by the War Department, marked the end of the "Indian wars."

When the great hunting cultures like the Plains Indians, Lakota and Cheyenne were confined to relatively tiny parcels of land called reservations, and the buffalo were deliberately shot almost to extinction, Indian men could no longer hunt, their great contribution to their tribes. In attempting to make Indian men self-reliant, and in a clumsy try at making life easier for Indian women, whites forced the former freedom-loving hunters into the dull life of farming after the European model. Indian men thus became farmers reluc-

tantly, simultaneously relieving their women of their ancient role as agriculturalists, their great source of pride and power. Under this genocidal attack on their culture, the power and status of native women went into steep decline. From this degeneration, they, along with their people, are now working to recover.

Despite colonization and Christianization, native people of all the nations quietly and secretly retained as much of their culture as they could. Today, across the continent, native people are openly participating in, rediscovering and taking pride in their traditions.

It is interesting to note that a recurring theme that echoed across native nations was the prophesying of the advent of the white man, or white brother; whether for good or ill was unknown. The Hopi of the West predicted this as did the Algonquian of the East. The current regeneration of Indian life was also foretold by Lakota elders during their darkest days in the late 1800s. Their holy ones knew that after a century of suffering, The People would begin to find their way again. As the prophecy foretold, The American Indian Movement, part of whose mission was to generate just such a rebirth, was founded approximately one hundred years after the telling of the prophecy.

Below: Oglala Lakota women line up for the beef issue on the Pine Ridge Reservation in this undated photograph, probably from the late nineteenth century. Restricted to the reservation, native men could no longer hunt for meat, and most of the buffalo had been killed by the late 1800s. The only meat available was the often wormy beef doled out by government agents. The rations were not welfare but part of the payment promised the Indians by treaty.

The people of the Six Nations Confederacy, also known as Iroquois, have retained as many of their old ways as was possible. An example of this may be seen in the 1990 siege at Oka, Canada, where Mohawks were surrounded by the military as they attempted to protect their aboriginal lands. Following tradition, the warrior society asked the permission of the women before "going to war." The women not only granted the permission, but joined their men at the front.

Kahn-tineta Horn, a strong activist among her people, went through the seventy-eight-day siege with them. When asked to speak as a native woman about the experience, she said, "Our duty according to our traditional law, our ways, is to stand beside the men when the land and people have to be defended. I went to Oka with two of my children, one was fourteen and the other was four, so they would remember what they saw and pass it down to their children. We did not want this to be forgotten."

THE ROLE OF EARLY WHITE HISTORIANS

White American historians from the mid-nineteenth to the mid-twentieth centuries also played a part in the denigration of native women's power. They did this by deliberately ignoring firsthand documentation in which Indian queens, or sunksquaws, are described as leaders of the East Coast peoples. In these "modern" histories, lengthy descriptions of the Delawares, for example, state that women could not be chiefs, that they sat in council only rarely. Some do not mention women at all, as if the female half of a race did not exist.

In point of fact, the early firsthand accounts note that there were many female leaders among the Algonquian peoples. George Fox, founder of Quakerism, a religion strong in its equal treatment of women, reported that "the old Empress sat in council," when he visited the Accomack Indians in 1673. In the early 1600s, the "Massachusetts Queen" governed the Massachusetts Confederacy. Weetamoo, the Pocasset sunksquaw, served as the war chief of Metacom, known to the Puritans as King Philip. She led three hundred warriors during Metacom's ultimately tragic conflict with the British in 1676. However, secondary documentation fails even to mention these female leaders.

THE GOVERNMENT REMOVAL POLICY

During the colonization period of the 1800s, the influence of Indian women was undermined deliberately by government agents. Men were given preference in education; in some cases, women were not educated at all. They were supposed to confine themselves to caring for the welfare of their nuclear family and stay out of politics—just like their white sisters.

An excellent example of this is what happened to the Cherokee, although the story would be repeated across the continent. Under relentless pressure to conform, Cherokee society, once based on the egalitarian matrilocal clan system, became highly patriarchal and stratified, mirroring the white society that surrounded it. In the early 1800s the Cherokee nation made a desperate attempt to stave off the U.S. government's "removal policy," which called for the Cherokee to be driven off their ancestral farms and deported to the wastelands of Oklahoma. Against the wishes of many of their women leaders, the male Cherokee leaders adopted a constitution based on that of the United States in which, among other things, women were disenfranchised. Reduced to chattel, Cherokee women had no official voice in the struggle to retain their lands.

Nanyehi, or Nancy Ward, was the last Beloved Woman, or head of the Council of Women, of her tribe. The Council was disbanded through the new constitution, and Nancy Ward was forced to resign her high office in 1817. The position had given her many powers, including the right to vote in the Chief's Council, decide the fate of captives and speak for the concerns of the women regarding

Below: Robert Lindneux's painting The Trail of Tears *captures the suffering of the Cherokee during their forced march from Georgia to Oklahoma in the bitter winter of 1839. In the government-enforced removal, about 4,000 Cherokees died on the 116-day journey due to the inadequate food supply and relentless pace.*

Above: *Smoking the peace pipe marks the end of important occasions both spiritual and temporal. In this June 1986 photograph, Wilma Mankiller (L), chief of the Cherokee Nation of Oklahoma, and Robert Youngdeer (R), chief of the Eastern Band of the Cherokee Indians, conclude a special joint session of their tribes.*

tribal matters. As her last political act, Nancy Ward begged the Council men not to agree to go to Oklahoma, using sentiments that would echo across Indian country through time and space.

"Cherokee mothers do not wish to go to an unknown country," she said. "We have raised all of you on the land we now have, which God gave us to inhabit. We have understood that some of our children wish to go over the Mississippi, but this act…would be like destroying your mothers. We beg of you not to part with any more of our land but keep it for our growing children for it was the good will of our creator to place us there."

Nancy did not live to see the sad day when the Cherokee were forced to leave their well-tended farms in the east and march west to Oklahoma along the bitter Trail of Tears. During that forced march, some of it in dead winter, many men, women and children perished to make room for the whites they had tried so hard to appease.

If she were alive today, Nancy Ward would be proud of the fact that Cherokee women not only have the right to vote in the elections of the Cherokee Nation, but a woman has also served several terms as the Nation's Principle Chief. An internationally renowned if somewhat controversial figure, Wilma Mankiller has devoted years of service to her Nation.

WE'RE STILL HERE!

Indian people have survived what may be considered the worst holocaust in history. Over a period of five hundred years, one hundred million Indians were killed by disease or war, and the survivors to this day are still subjected to every form of abuse and manipulation. The reservation system was so successful that when searching for an answer to his "Jewish problem," Hitler turned to the American treatment of Indians for inspiration. To have allowed them to survive under such extreme abuse, the spiritual values of The People had to be strong and true.

In North and South America, New Zealand, Australia and other places around the globe, indigenous, woman-centered cultures have managed to survive to this day. Their populations may be comparatively small but their voices are growing on the international scene. They conduct meetings under United Nations auspices with NGO (nongovernmental organization) status, and convene international indigenous conferences to discuss pressing global issues such as rain forest depredation that face not only their peoples, but all of humanity.

Left: Native American women remain a central source of strength for their families despite great strain on their way of life. With great flexibility they have managed to adapt to the new ways while retaining much of the old.

THE FEMALE POWERS

See the woman she has a young face an old face she carries herself well in all ages she survives all man has done in some tribes she is free in some religions she is under man….see the woman beauty…see the woman spirit daily serving courage with laughter…
— FROM "SEE THE WOMAN" BY JOHN TRUDELL,
   SANTEE ACTIVIST, POET

Opposite: *An Eskimo woman from Wood Island. She seems to be looking toward the uncertain future with a strong, unwavering gaze.*

SPIRITUAL POWER

Unlike Westerners, native peoples see life as one continuous living whole in which everything is connected and everything is alive. The earth itself is alive. Lakota people end prayers saying, *Mitakuye Oyasin*, "all my relations," meaning "we are all related."

Native people do not believe that woman or man needs a mediator to speak for her or him to the Great Mystery, the great generative force behind all life. Many Indians, such as the Hopi, believe that humans were placed on Earth not to rule it but to take care of it; to be, as it were, gardeners in paradise. Taking care of Earth includes practicing rituals and ceremonies to celebrate the different stages of life of individuals in the tribe, give thanks for blessings given the people or humbly ask the chiefs of the plant and animal spirits to send their people to the tribe once again, that the humans might be fed for another year.

With most adult women in their prime fully occupied by the raising of children, the care of families and the tending of agriculture, men often performed certain of these rituals. Many tribes understand that herbal and spiritual remedies lose their power if dispensed by a menstruating woman, for the nature of her life-giving Powers may clash with the Powers that bring healing. Yet the women had sacred rites that only they could perform and women's societies through which they gathered strength and gave direction to the nation.

The strongest example of women who have played a direct part in the rituals of the spiritual life of their tribe are the Blackfoot of Canada. Blackfoot women are the keepers of the most sacred medicine bundles that protect the life and health of The People. It is the women who open the bundles, and it is they who hand sacred objects to the men for ceremonial use. They evoke the spirits. Their presence is required for every ceremony, most especially the annual Sun Dance. While the Blackfoot women may have played a comparatively larger role in the spiritual life of their nation, the women of all Indian nations had their parts to play, their societies and their ritual observances.

Some ceremonies in which men conducted the prayers and rituals did exclude women. In some nations, the sweat lodge, where body and soul are purified, were used by men only. It was considered the male version of the four-day purification period during which women menstruate. Today, both men and women participate in sweat lodges, called Inipi by the Lakota, although segregation by sex is preferred.

There are also tribal ceremonies conducted by men that require the presence of a woman for the ritual to be complete. Today among traditionalist Plains Indians, the drum, considered the heartbeat of the Earth, is played as it has always been by men seated around it in a circle. Standing behind them, the women sing along with the men, their high-pitched voices adding drama and balance. As in all aspects of life, native people are aware of the need for balance, and this includes the balance between male and female.

Right: *This elder Blackfoot woman, Makah, is a member of the sacred Motokiks, a female society. She wears a headdress of buffalo horns and feathers. The eagle-bone whistle in her mouth was blown during the sacred dances of the Motokiks. Photograph by Edward S. Curtis, circa 1900.*

Left: *This Hopi priestess carries a sacred wand. Photograph by Charles Carpenter, circa 1898–1905. While most native healers were men, the women of many tribes could become healers or holy people after they had had their families. Once banned by law in the United States, many of the ancient methods are still in quiet use today.*

MEDICINE POWER

Anthropologists have believed that most Indian medicine men were exactly that: men. However, Native author Paula Gunn Allen writes of the Anishinabeg (Chippewa/Ojibwa) and their midewi-win, or "medicine dance," that to her resembles the mystery schools of the ancient Mediterranean cultures through which the divine was sought. She believes that all of the chief practitioners and teachers of this sacred native school were women. By extension, she also believes that women played a far greater role in the spiritual lives of most Indian nations than is presently supposed.

Ms. Allen backs up her argument by pointing to the fact that early history texts and observations were written by European men who, because of cultural bias, could not or would not comprehend and acknowledge female spiritual power when they saw it. And if they did see it, the natural instinct on the part of most of them would be to suppress it as being "against the natural order of things." During the early invasion period on the American continent, it must be remembered that in Europe the last medicine people, the female "witches," were being burned at the stake or otherwise murdered. The religious male hierarchy was determined to keep the upper hand in both the New and the Old Worlds.

Most native women understood the basic use of herbs for simple healing and cleansing, a sort of first aid kit for the family. But to become a true medicine person, a woman or man had to undergo years of rigorous training. The knowledge of herbs and the way in which they had to be picked, treated, dried and used, alone or in combination with other herbs, was extensive and exacting. Many of the powerful healing herbs that native people once relied upon are no longer in existence due to pollution and the intensive cultivation of formerly wild soils.

Indian people understood that there is a spiritual and emotional component to any illness, and thus the true healer had to be wise to the ways of the human heart, an ability with which many women are naturally gifted.

An example of this holistic approach to healing may be seen in the story of an Indian woman known to the author who suffered terribly from asthma to the point where she was forced to drag a tank of oxygen about with her wherever she went. This miserable situation continued for some time, until her family turned to a traditional medicine woman for help. The first thing the medicine woman did was gather the entire extended family together. In the discussion that ensued, many feelings were brought out and discussed, and this formed the basis of the healing. The medicine woman then treated the sick woman with herbs, and in less than one month, she was free of the oxygen tanks. Today, her health has been completely restored.

Beverly Hungry Wolf writes of her grandmother, Otsani, who was adept at using cactus spines and porcupine quills in much the same manner as Chinese doctors use acupuncture. This grandmother had the power to communicate with ghosts in order to find lost objects. Ms. Hungry Wolf relates how a cousin, having lost his knife, brought the traditional gift of tobacco to the medicine woman, who, upon accepting the tobacco, agreed to help him find his knife. With the lights out, she called upon her ghost, offered it gifts of food, and requested its help. When the lights came back on, the food was gone and the knife lay on the floor at their feet.

Traditional native people approach supernaturals with great respect and caution, because they truly believe in their existence. It is understood that these beings are more powerful than, and are not controllable by, human beings. To become a medicine person who can deal with The Powers requires study, discipline and extensive training. This is why New Agers who play at being medicine people are viewed with alarm by native people.

CYCLES AND POWERS

Traditional native men consider the ability of women to bear children the greatest human power of all. During menstruation, as the female body prepares for new life, this power is at its height. At this time, the power is so strong that it can cancel or otherwise interfere with the spiritual power that a medicine man must call upon to effect a healing. Thus, a menstruating woman traditionally avoids the presence of a medicine man for the protection of them both.

As with other native traditions and rituals, the isolation of women during menses is based upon common sense. Menses is understood as a time of purification for women. The Yurok women of northwestern California regard menstrual blood as a purifying force, cleansing the womb of all extraneous materials including dead male sperm, thus preparing the womb for the advent of new life. They believe that menstruation is a time to rest and regain spiritual energy.

It was typical in most tribes for women to live apart from the family and band or village during the first four days of menstruation. Among the Lakota, they rested in a separate lodge, where their needs were often attended to by young girls. In other nations, a separate part of the family tipi or lodge was set aside for them. Before a woman could become a true medicine or holy person, she had to go through menopause. After menopause, many new duties and privileges were open to her as she entered a new and uniquely vital time of life.

Above: In a village on the Hopi Reservation in Arizona, girls work at basket weaving in this 1903 photograph. Adolescent Hopi girls traditionally wear their hair in this style until marriage.

Right: This photograph shows setup for the puberty ceremony for Hollow Horn Bear's daughters, circa 1893. Traditionally, when a young Lakota woman came of age, her father announced the fact from the entrance to his lodge. The celebrant was then dressed in her finest clothing and stood just inside the tipi to be seen by all. Guests feasted and quietly discussed the virtues of the child who had become a woman.

Women were not alone in having to spend time away from the group during a period of purification. In many nations, warriors returning from combat underwent periods of ritual purification before they could re-enter the village or have sexual intercourse.

THE SUN DANCE

The sacred Sun Dance is a ceremony in which menstruating women aren't present, once again because of female powers that would conflict with the powers of the males. A non-Indian friend of the author's recently attended a Sun Dance in which everything went wrong until the medicine man leading the ceremony determined that two menstruating women were present. The women were politely asked to leave, and the ceremony proceeded with no further disturbance.

The Sun Dance is a male-centered ceremony which began among the Plains Indians and is now practiced by many Native peoples. It is held at the height of summer, not, as was supposed by European missionaries who banned the ceremony, to literally worship the sun, but to honor the women and celebrate the power of fertility. (One might view the workings of life as Father Sun impregnating Mother Earth with his warm, powerful rays.)

During the ceremony, the Sun Dancing men abstain from all food and water and dance around the sacred tree for four days, always facing the sun from sunup to sundown. During the dance, their chests are pierced by sticks that are tied by ropes to the sacred tree, from which they must pull free. The men are surrounded by family and friends, supporters who dance and pray with them "for all The People."

Women may make flesh offerings during this time, cutting small pieces of skin from their arms. In some cases today, women have also been pierced, usually in the back or on the upper arms, as a sacrifice to ask blessings upon the nation.

The Sun Dance provides many benefits for the participants. Healings take place during this four-day ritual. Requests are made in prayer. Sun Dancers may offer thanks for a request that has been granted by the Great Mystery during the past year.

At its deepest level, the Sun Dance allows men to understand the sacrifice and pain of childbirth through which their women must go. Here again, harmony is sought, and women as the creators of life are deeply honored. Through a physically and spiritually demanding ritual sacrifice, the male seeks to come into balance with the female.

RITES OF PASSAGE

A young girl's first menses was treated as a time of ritual initiation into womanhood. Life changed for a carefree young girl, sometimes quite dramatically. She had to behave with more poise and reserve, no longer playing with her brothers and running wild in the fields. Her serious role as a future mother of the nation was upon her, and she had to put aside childish things.

In most tribes, there were public acknowledgements that this rite of passage had occurred. Navajo and Apache tribes held elaborate ceremonies that lasted for days, during which many guests were feasted. A northwest coast Tlingit father would host a potlatch, a giveaway, in honor of his daughter's becoming a woman. A Cheyenne or Lakota father would give away a favorite horse, announcing his daughter's new role in the tribe from the door of his tipi.

Left: The Hopi women's dance, done in a circle. This 1879 photograph, taken in Oraibi, Arizona, gives an unusual aerial view.

RAISING THE NEXT GENERATION

There is an old saying that it takes a whole village to raise a child. This was true among Indian people, whether they lived in the mobile hunting bands of the Plains, in the longhouses of the northeast or in settled pueblos of the southwest.

Luther Standing Bear of the Lakota, born just before the end of his people's great horse culture, writes of the gentle patience of his mother, who never scolded him for mistakes, but always praised him when he did well, fostering in him a desire to please her. As a child, he felt completely safe inside the village because he knew that all the women in the band were in a sense his aunts. Every adult felt responsible for every child, indeed for every person. As long as one cooking pot was full, no one ever went hungry. And no child was ever left alone. Cradle boards protected babies and allowed mothers to take their infants along as they went about their daily tasks.

Artistic and other traditions were passed on to children by allowing them to observe mothers and fathers at their daily work. In the Indian way, youngsters learned by observation and personal trial and error, not by lecture. When the children did well in their imitation of grownup skills, adults praised them mightily. If a young lady among the Plains people created a beautiful dress, a proud mother might hang it upon a bush close to a well-used path to be admired by passersby.

Indian children of the Plains were given small versions of the implements that their parents used, much as toys are given to children today, but always with a serious purpose in mind. Boys were given small bows and arrows with which to begin practicing their hunting skills. Girls often had miniature tipis to play in (as well as girl-sized cooking utensils to go inside), helping the women of the family stretch, clean and tan the hides that made the tipi covering. In this way they learned the skills they would need as adults.

Indian parents were horrified at the methods whites used to teach children. They could not fathom the cruelty of the punishments forcibly administered on their own children at the white boarding schools that proliferated during the reservation era, and to which Indian families had, by law, to send their young.

The infamous Bureau of Indian Affairs boarding schools were designed to turn Indian children into imitations of obedient little "white ladies and gentlemen." The educational philosophy was to "kill the Indian and save the man." The children's long hair, of which they were so proud, was cut off. Their easy-fitting, graceful leather clothes were exchanged for starched high collars and stiff-laced boots. They were physically punished for speaking their native languages.

Left: In Montana, a Plains mother holds up her infant to be blessed by the rays of the rising sun. Arising early to greet the sun was part of traditional life across the continent. Lakota Luther Standing Bear spoke of catching the energy provided by the atmosphere of dawn.

Indeed, little respect was shown to the children, and none to the cultures of their families. Often kept from home for years, they returned to their reservations unable to fit into the old world and yet not truly fitted to work successfully in the new white world. The schools did nothing to nurture the self-confidence and values that enable young people to grow strong and create solid families of their own upon reaching adulthood. Native people see this as one more way in which white society has attempted to break down their traditions and their nations. A broken nation is less able to defend itself against further encroachments by the dominant society upon what lands the nation has left by right of treaty.

Traditional Indian education, on the other hand, created strong, loyal tribal members who were able and encouraged to think and speak for themselves. Indians had what educators today would consider a very enlightened view of education.

Right: A Kiowa girl holds a toy cradle board and doll. Toy versions of real implements helped children learn skills they would need in adult life.

In raising their young, women took great care to protect the will and sense of self of each child, at the same time teaching the child by example to show respect to others. Young people were expected to grow up with the ability to direct their own lives, think for themselves and not merely to take orders from others as whites were (and still are) trained to do, both at home and at school. Only with a good sense of self could a child show the respect and caring for others so necessary for a people highly interdependent for sheer physical survival. Adults with the ability to think for themselves were more capable of responding creatively and flexibly to changes in the natural world. Today, traditionalist native women still raise their children in this manner.

Ella Deloria of the Yankton Lakota speaks of how a child's correction, when administered, tended to be given indirectly, so as not to offend or belittle, but get the point across. If a child misbehaved, mother might simply ignore the young one, praising another who was behaving. She might even pretend to scold an older child, one who understood that she was part of mother's lesson plan, so that the little one would hear the lesson without being personally humiliated by it.

In a tribal society where the people lived close to the elements and were dependent upon the Earth and its moods and seasons, it was imperative to raise physically robust, personally self-confident women and men who could take on the role of caring for the old and raising the next generation when it came their turn. By contrast, in white society, where obedience to authority was of paramount importance and where imitative rather than innovative thinking was required in an industrializing society, very different methods of child raising were employed.

In *These Were The Sioux*, Mari Sandoz, a white woman who grew up on a homestead in the Sandhills of Nebraska, wrote movingly about the Indians whose children she played with while growing up. "I still remember the closed, distant faces of the (adult) Sioux when I was whipped for staying out to watch the *heyoka* (Indian sacred clown) in the thunderstorm, and at other whippings as well. The American Indian considered the whites a brutal people who treated their children like enemies—playthings, too, coddling them like pampered pets or fragile toys, but underneath like enemies to be restrained, bribed, spied on, and punished, or as objects of competition between the parents, sometimes even to open quarrelings and worse over them. The Indians believed that children so treated could only grow up dependent and immature pets and toys, but with adult wills and appetites to be indulged—grow up designing, angered and dangerous enemies within the family circle, to be appeased and fought and be defeated, perhaps even murdered. The Indians pointed to the increasing lawlessness and violence of the young people of the white man, a violence that was

Left: This photograph of nuns with their Indian pupils was taken at the Sisters of the Child Jesus, St. Joseph's Mission in British Columbia, circa 1900. Both the United States and Canada attempted to deal with their "Indian problems" through complete and harshly enforced assimilation. Some children were taken from their parents at a very young age and raised in boarding schools.

often turned against their elders. Such a thing was unknown among the tribes in the old days and very rare up to the recent expropriating days, when so many thousands of Indians were driven off their small holdings on the reservations into an alien society."

THE POWER OF THE ELDERS

In modern American society, old people are often considered of limited use or relevance. In a society in which scientific advances bring new changes and, in effect, new worlds with each passing day, elders are incapable of being repositories of the kind of knowledge prized in an industrial world. Among aboriginal peoples who live in an indigenous world, a type of wisdom is prized that can only be gained by having lived life and observed it well, and from understanding the timeless depths of human nature. In this world, elders are regarded as a most precious resource.

For Native American women, the end of the childbearing years marks a transition into a new world of respect and power. Older women often assume new ritual duties. In many societies, when spiritually gifted women reached post-menopausal age, they were eligible to become medicine or holy people. Most women of child-

Right: An elder woman of the Nakoaktok. She is carefully decorating a hat using traditional patterns of the Northwest Coast tribes. Elders are highly respected as the repositories of ancient tribal lore and time-tested wisdom.

bearing age had cares and responsibilities that would inhibit their effective practice of this additional service to their nation.

Female elders were, and are, valued as the keepers of tribal history. During a typical day in a village, the young women went about their varied tasks, gathering wild foods, cultivating domesticated ones, butchering and drying the meat that their husbands brought in from the hunt and scraping and tanning the hides from which they then made clothes and other household items. It fell to the grandmothers to look after the little ones, making sure that they had all they wanted to eat from the cooking pot. Grandmothers taught the children the ancient tribal creation stories, the clan songs and took them for walks in the woods to find secret places where the healing herbs lived.

Today, it is still custom and a point of pride among Indian peoples to show respect for their elders that is not observed in the "modern" world. At powwows and other social gatherings, the first shady spots under the arbor are reserved for the old people and the children. At feasts, elders and young children are the first to be served, while the strong may help themselves to what is left.

A recent illustration of this idea in action occurred in the formation of the American Indian Movement (AIM). While AIM was founded mostly by young city Indians, they relied heavily upon the elders when formulating principles and strategies. The organization was established to revive Indian pride and focus Indian nations on regaining their sovereignty. It stood for self-determination for the nations, not just the self-administration policies handed down to tribal governments by the Bureau of Indian Affairs (BIA). Elder women are credited with providing the initial impetus to found that organization dedicated to reclaiming Indian rights and the resurrection of Indian pride.

POLITICAL POWER — PAST

At the time of invasion, the political power of native women varied from one nation to the next. But as the creative, life-giving force of their people, almost all native women were treated with much higher regard and had greater freedoms than did their European sisters of the same time period.

One of the best examples of matrilocal native societies was to be found among the Iroquois, the famous Confederacy of the Six Nations: Seneca, Mohawk, Onondaga, Tuscarora, Cayuga and Oneida. With a vast territory that stretched from what is now New York State to Ontario, Canada, they first came into contact with whites in the mid-seventeenth century.

Six Nations women held great political power through the female leaders of the clans. The clans lived in longhouses, each of which was organized and run by a respected elder woman. Under the matrilocal system, the husband moved in with his wife's family, much as with the Lakota, Keres and Navajo people. Powerful elder women became the heads of villages, which were groups of long-houses. It was these women who selected the men who would represent the people at village and tribal councils and at the great council of the Six Nations Confederacy.

Women were the custodians of the antler headdresses, the signs of office for councilmen, and they could revoke these if the men proved unworthy of their sacred trust. The women were in charge of domestic affairs as well, not only owning the fields, but the long-houses where their families lived. In case of divorce, they had charge of their children. It was they who made the decisions as to when to plant and when to harvest the corn, beans, squash and the fruit from fields and orchards.

Besides hunting, the men were concerned primarily with the external affairs of state, but even here, no major decisions were made without the council and agreement of the women. As provided for in the Law of the Great Peace of the Iroquois Confederacy, women owned the tribal lands.

The Cherokee are another example of an Indian nation in which the women traditionally played a strong political role. European men saw the Cherokee men as living "under a petticoat government," because of the existence and influence of the powerful Women's Council. The head of the Council was called the Beloved Woman of the Nation, "whose voice was considered that of the Great Spirit, speaking through her." Under the influence of these petticoats, the nation set the penalty for killing a woman at twice that for killing a man. The Indians perceived that if a woman were killed, her unborn were in effect murdered with her. There is speculation that this doubling of the penalty was widespread among Indian nations before the influence of patriarchal Europeans.

POLITICAL POWER—PRESENT

The United States has not shown me the terms of my surrender.
—MARIE LEGO, PIT RIVER NATION, 1970

I try to tell our young people that if it wasn't for our women, we would not remain a distinct people. I want the world to know, my children to know, what our women have done. They're not squaws, man, they're heroes.
—RUSSELL MEANS, OGLALA LAKOTA PATRIOT, 1995

Left: Wounded Knee Village, shown at left, was the site of the 1890 massacre of 300 people. In 1973, Lakota patriots took over the village. In this 1973 photograph, Indian militants escort Harlington Wood, the assistant attorney general, from a meeting with leaders of the American Indian Movement.

Native women continue to play a pivotal role in the political renaissance of native people on this continent. They are to be found in the forefront of the native struggle to retain what lands have been left to them.

Women were instrumental in the founding and grass roots growth of the American Indian Movement. They took part in the demonstrations and were part of the leadership for such major standoffs as the confrontation on the Pine Ridge Reservation in 1973, when AIM activists took over the hamlet of Wounded Knee, declaring it free Indian country by treaty right. Among other things, the Indians demanded that the federal government review its broken treaties. The government responded by surrounding the tiny hamlet with the largest land army mustered by the U.S. government since the Civil War. A seventy-one-day standoff ensued.

During this difficult time, the women in the Wounded Knee camp were very strong. Having been instrumental in the founding of the American Indian Movement, native women represented at least half of the people present, standing by the men during the siege. Lakota elders Gladys Bissonnette and Ellen Moves Camp played instrumental roles, taking part in the days-long negotiations with U.S. government officials that finally ended the standoff.

The American press gave credit for the standoff and other dramatic demonstrations of Indian determination almost exclusively to male Indian leaders such as Russell Means and Dennis Banks. Along with the public credit, however, Indian men had to bear the brunt of government repression. One example of this is what came to be known as the Wounded Knee Leadership Trials. While male leadership was tied up in court or in prison, women carried on the struggle from the grass roots to the international level.

In 1926, Gertrude Simmons Bonnin (Lakota), formed the National Council of American Indians, a major Indian lobbying group that

Right: Native American women have always been at the forefront of the movement to protest the misuse and misappropriation of land.

is still in existence today. She became the organization's president and her husband was its secretary. She and Alice Lee Jemison (Seneca), set the stage for the increasing presence of Indian women in the political movements of the 1960s. While there are still many problems to be overcome, the past twenty years have seen a dramatic resurgence of Indian pride and culture, as exemplified in the many Indian organizations that promote Indian rights and guard Indian treaties, as well as in the culturally relevant economic development that is taking place, however slowly, on many Indian reservations.

As expounded by M. Annette Jaimes in *The State of Native America,* Indian women have responded to the problem of white-influenced sexism on the part of their men with a uniquely Indian solution. They have formed the political equivalent of traditional women's societies to regain their own strength and work as partners with their men in the common cause of their nations. In 1981, Yet Si Blue, also called Janet McCloud (Tulalip), longtime fishing rights activist and great-grandmother, formed the Northwest Indian Women's Circle. The Indigenous Women's Network, IWN, was founded by well-known activists Winona LaDuke (Mississippi Band Anishinabe) and Ingrid Wasinawatok-El Issa (Menominee). Indigenous Women's Network publishes the journal *Indigenous Woman.* Founding members of The International Indian Treaty Council included many native women of the American Indian Movement. The 1990s have been declared the Decade of Indigenous

Peoples. Delphine Red Shirt (Lakota) currently chairs the NGO Committee on the International Decade of the World's Indigenous Peoples. She devotes herself to the work in the spirit of an ancient tenet of her people: that the strong and able are duty bound to protect and care for the helpless ones.

Native women today find themselves between two worlds, and many walk the line between them with admirable grace. An excellent example is the case of Dr. Cupp, a Navajo surgeon, who has returned home to practice on her reservation. She was the inspiration behind the traditional healing room in the Navajo hospital where medicine men can work with traditionalist patients. The first Navajo woman to become a surgeon, Dr. Cupp is following

Left: On January 30, 1990, Selba Walker, director of the Columbus Native American Indian Center, led a march to protest a bill that would make Indian remains in unmarked graves state property. Today it is illegal to disturb the remains of native people.

in the ground-breaking footsteps of the first American Indian doctor, Susan La Flesche Picotte, an Omaha, who lived in the 1850s.

Today, native women make significant contributions in a wide array of professions. They are lawyers, economists, teachers, as well as political leaders, activists and doctors. They also live in the poorer sections of urban ghettos, working with city Indian children who have perhaps never been to the reservation. The Heart of the Earth Schools had their beginnings in the early 1970s in a storefront in Minneapolis, Minnesota. Today, they may be found across the country. The curriculum is part American and part Native American. Each day begins in the traditional manner, with a daybreak ceremony at which sage (incense) is burned and drums are played. Along with English, native children study their own indigenous languages—on computers. At noon, the elders arrive to teach the children the ancient arts of beadwork, hide tanning, all the things that used to be done when the nations lived free. Unlike the BIA boarding schools, Heart of the Earth gives students a strong, secure sense of identity as well as a firm foundation of schooling to fit them for life in America today. It helps them live in a society that is industrial as opposed to indigenous.

Right: Susette La Flesche was the sister of Susan La Flesche, the first female American Indian physician. Susette was an ardent activist, lecturing audiences in America and Europe on the theft of Indian lands and the corruption of government agents. For these lectures she usually wore traditional Omaha ceremonial clothing.

Native American Survival Schools take children out of their urban settings into the wilderness of their ancestors. There they are taught to live as their ancestors did, putting up tipis, tapping maple trees, learning to live off the land. This helps the coming generation of children understand and maintain their traditional values. Women play a vital role in all of these educational activities. And many native women still live simple, quiet lives on back woods reservations, close to the earth as their great-great-grand-mothers once did, keeping the fires of tradition burning.

Above: An AIM rally in Pierre, South Dakota, on October 31, 1974. Founded in the late 1960s, the American Indian Movement was most active during the 1970s.

NATIVE WOMEN AND THE FEMINIST MOVEMENT
The difference between native women and white feminists is that the feminists talk about their rights and we talk about our responsibilities. There is a profound difference. Our responsibility is to take care of our natural place in the world.
—RENEE SENOGLES, RED LAKE CHIPPEWA

Suffragists such as Susan B. Anthony and Alice Fletcher noted how life enjoyed by Indian women differed strongly from that of American women. Iroquois society in New York State offered these reformers a chance to observe the life of Iroquois women. It is no accident that the suffragist movement was started in New York State.

Nancy Lurie, anthropologist and adopted Winnebago, wrote: "Whether the cosseted darling of the upper class or the toil-worn pioneer farm wife, the white woman was pitifully dependent through life on the whims and fortunes of one male, first a father and then a husband. Bereft of virtually any political rights, she also lacked the security of a tribe who would then be committed to care for her if she were orphaned or widowed. Traditionally, the poor white woman was left with the denigrating embarrassment of accepting charity."

While the white feminist movement in America owes a great debt to the example of personal freedoms and the strength demonstrated by native women, many native women do not agree with the current values and focus of the Women's Movement. As members of an oppressed minority, they view the rejection of their men as but one more in a long line of destructive divisions that have weakened once strongly unified nations.

Native women and men have a view of female power and strength that contrasts rather sharply with today's Women's Movement image. "The Eurocentric male will not recognize women, indigenous or otherwise, as being a valuable force in humanity. The only time he will recognize a woman is if she becomes a poor facsimile of a white man. He will allow the woman to remain a physical woman, but not a spiritual woman. If women enter the board rooms of corporate America and make the same kinds of decisions—even more vicious than the board chairmen—or if they pilot jet planes on the front lines, then they're recognized as being equal. And that's where I fault the feminist movement," writes Russell Means.

Rebecca Adamson is President of First Nations Development Institute, a research, policy reform and funding organization located near Washington, D.C. It was founded fifteen years ago and is dedicated to private sector, culturally viable development of reservation economies. In a speech to the Ms. Foundation in June of 1990, Ms. Adamson spoke of the need for more women to assume leadership positions and employ the values long associated with traditional native women. The following are excerpts from that speech.

"I am a *da gali* woman. *Da gali* means 'real people,' better known as Cherokee. As a Cherokee woman, you are expected to be a leader. In fact, for hundreds and hundreds of years, the wise women's White Council, (the Givers of Life), ruled the tribe in concert with the wise men's Red Council, (the Protectors of Life). It was not until the mid-1800s that federal agents from the Bureau of Indian Affairs forced women out of their rightful positions of leadership. By selecting only men to be on the council, conferring only with men, and distributing federal money, food and blankets only to men, the federal government was able to shift the balance of power within our people. No longer were women the 'givers of life,' the enablers, the nurturers, recognized leaders. Our people suffered.

"Well, I can't accept this. As a Cherokee woman, I was raised to use my power to lead. I am responsible for the Earth and my children. We all must collectively use the power of women and lead our country out of this dark age of man's manifest destiny into a more humane, ecologically sane future.

"The careful research and development process that we employ at First Nations, which involves listening and responding to the ideas of the grassroots people, is missing from governmental funding agencies that want quick fixes. These agencies could learn from and use the more far-seeing Third World sense of time as they develop projects and begin funding.

"Today's politicians, economists, and academics don't have the solutions. We women are the practical visionaries. Let's go back to the Cherokee lesson, conferring, sharing information, and bringing women into economic networks. Let us be audacious leaders and assume the responsibility for life. Let us dare to think in new, imaginative, and creative ways to make profound change."

Left: A tipi (possibly Blackfoot) on the grounds of the Washington Monument. In this July 1978 rally, over five hundred Indians marched across the United States and staged a week-long protest to pressure the government to respond to Native American issues.

BELOVED WOMAN EARTH

In our religion, we look at this planet as a woman. She is the most important female to us because she keeps us alive. We are nursing off of her.
——MARY GOPHER, OJIBWA

*This land is the house
we have always lived in.
The women,
their bones are holding up the earth.*
——FROM "CALLING MYSELF HOME," LINDA HOGAN,
   CHICKASAW POET

The men who are brought up to respect women, the men who are brought up to respect the earth as woman, think of the earth and the woman as one and the same, are the real men. Everything that gives birth is female. When men begin to understand the relationships of the universe that women have always known, the world will begin to change for the better.
——LORRAINE CANOE, MOHAWK ELDER

Opposite: A mother and daughter tend their field on the Navajo Reservation.

MISTRESSES OF THE SOIL

Native women were America's first farmers. They owned the fields they cultivated, as well as the proceeds therefrom, and passed them on to their daughters. They were also America's first geneticists, experimenting with different strains of plants, domesticating the wild weeds that they came upon in their early hunter-gatherer days, developing them into plants such as corn, beans, squash, potatoes, peanuts, peppers, sunflowers and tomatoes. This was not only of critical value to their own societies, but ultimately to Europe and the wider world as well, as the plants that native women developed in the "new" world literally rejuvenated the old. Along with food crops, native women developed plants from which dyes were made, plants which traditional Navajo weavers still use today to dye their rugs and weavings. As well, women discovered and fostered medicinal plants, many of which form the basis of the current pharmaceutical industry.

While the men focused on hunting and fishing, the agricultural activities of the women often provided as much as 80 percent of their family's food supply. This fact went a long way to contributing to the status of women in Native American societies, which was especially high in comparison to their European female contemporaries. This is proven by the drastic change that took place during the settlement period, when Indian men took over the farming role and the status of women went into decline.

But prior to European invasion, in almost all nations, women were held in great esteem. A Seneca-Cayuga orator was noted to have said in an address to New York governor George Clinton in 1788, "Our ancestors considered it a great offense to reject the counsels of their women, particularly that of female governesses. They were esteemed the mistresses of the soil. Who, said they, bring us into being? Who cultivates our land, kindles our fires, but our women?"

As in most nations, Iroquois women owned the family dwelling and its contents, along with the fields and the produce derived therefrom. They worked cooperatively to cultivate the fields, often under the direction and guidance of an elder woman. While the younger women worked, the grandmothers watched the children. Young girls were taught farming from an early age, given seeds to

Right: At the San Ildefonso Pueblo, women hang chile to dry. Photograph by T. Harmon Parkhurst.

Above: A Maidu woman
of California cooks acorn
mush circa 1900.

plant and praised when they cooked meals from the produce they had grown. The men would no more think of concerning themselves with cultivation than they would of assuming ownership of the family dwelling, the longhouse, since all property including the fields belonged to the maternal lineage group. Upon marriage, an Iroquois man went to live with his wife's clan. Everything, including their children, belonged to his wife, except his weapons and the personal possessions that he brought with him to the marriage. Choosing the best leaders in the interests of The People, Clan mothers appointed and dismissed all clan chiefs.

Women controlled Iroquois society for good reason. The men as hunters and traders were often away from home. A war party might take a husband away for months at a time. The women were left to be defended by a small party of men, and beyond that, child and plant care were in the hands of the women. This matrilineal clan system was to develop into the great Iroquois League of six nations, the powerful northeastern tribes who dominated the area from the Adirondacks to the Great Lakes. Developed with its laws and customs well before white contact, it was to have a strong influence upon the development of the United States Constitution.

THE BEGINNINGS OF AGRICULTURE

Agriculture of a type was woven into the earliest times of human hunter-gatherer life. Native women would help a crop along, ensuring that a stand of wild grasses, turnips or a fruit tree would be

Opposite: An Edward S. Curtis photograph of women, probably Apache, in Arizona. The enormous bowls could be used to carry food or as a sunshade.

Below: Gathering Wild Rice. *This 1884 engraving depicts native women harvesting a type of grass. Wild rice is now popular around the world.*

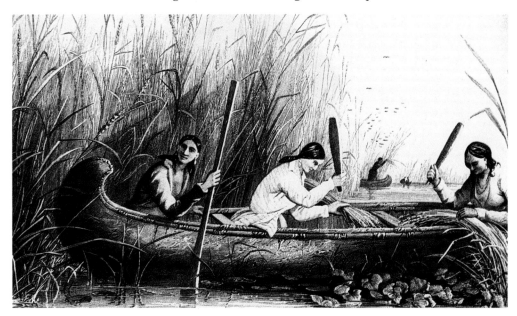

healthy and ready for harvest when the band returned on its migratory route through its hunting lands. When agriculture became more seriously relied upon and crops failed due to drought or blight, native women knew where to find the wild foods that often grew in quiet, secret places. All of this meant that native women had to be very flexible, able to alter their way of life, staying attuned to the conditions of their natural surroundings.

The Apache, who moved about a great deal, provide an excellent example of this native ability to adapt and go with nature. They hunted, taking just enough to feed their families. The women planted small gardens, enough to feed the group and no more, which meant that they were neither attached to any particular spot of land nor were they eager to acquire more than they needed at any given time. They, like other Indians, understood crop rotation, and let land lie fallow while they moved on to cultivate other gardens.

As with other tribes, farming was the work of Apache women. The men might assist, but the women were perceived to be better at it, and it was their responsibility. The women knew the rituals involved in planting, and prayed while they worked. Several thou-

Below: Two Walapai women carrying water pouches.

sand years ago, when agriculture finally took firm hold in the Southwest, the people turned to it exclusively, leaving the hunting-gathering life behind. Because the reliance on agriculture was exclusive, and thus high-risk, the women had to develop the technological skill to ensure that it was successful.

The desert-dwelling farmers built hundreds of miles of irrigation canals throughout central Arizona. The modern city of Phoenix has literally imposed its canal system atop that of the early Hohokam people, who lived in the area from AD 200 to 1450. It is thought that the modern-day Pima and Papago peoples are descended from the technologically advanced Hohokam.

While the critical importance of crop diversity is just beginning to be understood by western agriculturalists, native people understood the concept and its value thousands of years ago. Ancient Peruvians brought crop experimentation to an art rarely matched in world history, developing different types of plants for every type of climactic condition, rather than attempting to suit the environment to the crop. At the time of the Spanish conquest, Andean farmers were producing three thousand varieties of potato. The Andean Indians even used a simple but effective method of freeze-drying the crop for long storage. Had the Irish understood crop diversity, the great potato blight of the mid-nineteenth century, which brought the death, social dislocation and exodus of millions, could have been lessened or possibly avoided altogether. The potato grew wild all through the Americas, and Indians of the southwestern United States, especially the Navajo, engaged in their own development of this crop.

Native women grew corn all across North America. It was a food staple upon which most nations depended. Among the Hopi and the Pueblo peoples, corn achieved a mystic significance. When a young Hopi girl comes of age, part of her ceremony includes being dusted with sacred golden corn pollen. While old world grains came in few varieties, Indians developed corn that could grow from Canada to Florida, in colors spanning yellow, red, blue and purple. It is estimated that over seven thousand years ago, Indians began to domesticate hundreds of kinds of maize, starting in Mexico with a common wild grass called *teosinte*. Originally, corn cobs were tiny, about the size of a woman's thumb. Corn was developed comparatively late in American agriculture—it followed the cultivation of squash and beans by about one thousand years.

Brought to Europe in the sixteenth century, crops like potato and corn had a dramatic and positive effect on the European population, the aftershocks of which resulted in tragedy for the native people of America. In Europe, the new foods dramatically improved general health as the rate of famine declined. The population began to burgeon. At the same time, under the growing influence of the male-dominated church, birth control practices, including variations on the rhythm method and the use of herbs to prevent inception or to cause early abortion, were becoming outlawed in Europe. The midwives who once understood these practices were burned at the stake in the great witch hunts. Tragically and ironically, this European population explosion was in part responsible for the massive western migrations that resulted ultimately in disaster for the New World's first inhabitants.

HILLING THE SOIL

As among many other nations, Iroquois social and ceremonial life centered on agriculture. They believed that soil would not bear fruit unless the women did the cultivating, and to promote this, female societies took part in fertility ceremonies to promote the growth of the crops.

In early spring, seeds were soaked, then started in the longhouses in rows of bark trays. As the season unfolded, the women worked together to plant, hoe, harvest and finally store their produce for the long winter. The Iroquoian crops included fifteen varieties of corn and as many as sixty types of beans, squash, potatoes, nuts and peppers. Women of the Seneca tribe were said to plant and harvest in one year over a million bushels of corn, tons of beans, squash and sunflower seeds. What was not used was stored in underground granaries.

While there are no ancient texts to document the case, it may be understood that, as the cultivators of their nations, women were heavily and continually engaged in crop experimentation and development. A claim may be made that Native American women developed the foods that today feed 70 percent of the world's population. Cotton and tobacco, crops upon which white men would later build huge fortunes, may also have been developed by native women to clothe their families and offer prayers to the Great Spirit or Great Mystery.

In the traditional native agricultural system, corn was planted in mounds in small fields. These small mounds, or hills, retained more soil than the European plowing and straight-line cultivation methods. As long as European settlers, having learned from their Indian neighbors, followed the practice of hilling, the soil remained stable.

Unfortunately, by the 1930s this practice was abandoned by the United States, and now thousands of tons of the best soils are

drained down the Mississippi River system every year. At this point, two-thirds of the golden soil that took millennia to build up is now forever lost. Added to the current use of pesticides and chemicals, which are now understood to reduce soil fertility, the ability of the American West to produce food crops is seriously threatened.

Native women were able to produce their crop yields through natural means. The ancient tradition of growing the "three sisters"—corn, beans and squash—together offers several advantages, including a corn yield that is increased by 50 percent. In this system, each plant grows better in concert with the other two than it would alone: the leaves of the corn plant shade the more delicate bean plants and the corn stalk provides a stake up which beans and squash vines grow. As squash vines cross the ground between the corn and bean plants, the earth is covered, preserving rain and soil and keeping out weeds. This method also reduces crop loss due to insects.

Above: Zuni *"waffle gardens" were an effective agricultural practice in an arid climate. Undated photograph, probably turn of the century.*

59

HEALTH AND HEALING

As anthropological data shows, native people, living as they did on fresh fruits and vegetables cultivated by their women, did not have the tooth decay and gum diseases that plagued Europeans. In Europe, wheat was the staple of the diet, and, unlike the corn and potatoes eaten in the Americas, this food stuck to the teeth, helping cause decay. Until the invasion, native elders tended to live to advanced ages, often over one hundred years, and they kept their teeth.

Weston Price, an American dentist born in 1870, noted that the teeth of his patient's children were weaker than those of their parents, and that their dental arches were more crowded. He suspected that changes in nutrition were responsible for this deterioration, and set out to test his theory.

Price knew that anthropologists had long observed that excellent teeth were to be found in primitive cultures. Fortunately, he was able to study the culture of indigenous peoples around the world at a time when there were still many people who lived that way. As well, he did his work at a time when photography had become available to help keep records and prove his data with visual aids.

Price examined aboriginal people around the world, taking thousands of photographs and keeping detailed records. He found whole cultures with neither tooth decay nor misshapen dental arches nor crowded teeth. He interviewed an American doctor who stated that in all his thirty-five years of practice, he had never seen a case of cancer among Eskimo and northern Indians provided they remained living on their traditional diet. However, as soon as Indians began to eat the white man's refined foods — sugar, white flour and canned foods — their health deteriorated, often rapidly. Tuberculosis was a major killer, but if patients returned to their native diet, they usually recovered.

The work of Dr. Price helps show that the life of preindustrial man was not the nasty, brutish and short existence of popular legend. Another trait that Price found as he got to know many of his Indian subjects had to do with the strength of their characters, a trait he came to associate with the diet and culture of First Peoples.

Price also discovered that native people knew which part of the animal provided the crucial vitamins that would prevent such diseases as scurvy. The Plains Indians ate raw adrenal glands, the small balls in the fat above each kidney, which scientists now understand contain the highest source of vitamin C in any tissue, plant or animal. Native women knew that these glands must be eaten raw (cooking kills the vitamin C), their wisdom predating the "discovery" of vitamin C by thousands of years.

Left: A woman of the Tsuu T'ina Nation in Alberta, Canada, drying food over a fire. This is an ancient and effective method of preserving meat, fish and vegetables.

Vitamin A is to be found in high concentrations in the fatty tissue around the eyes of an animal. This the native women also avoided cooking. For nine months of the year, the nutrition of Plains Indians, and certainly that of the Eskimo, Inuit and other circumpolar peoples, was confined to wild game. Thus, emphasis was placed on eating internal organs, including the wall of certain sections of the digestive tract. Bone marrow was prized. The thyroid gland was also eaten raw.

Native women who sought to get pregnant ate extra thyroid glands from animals to assist in fertility. Plains women made nutritious pemmican by pounding up dried beef and bone marrow with berries high in vitamin C and combining this mixture with fat. Pemmican was excellent and portable food for hunters on the move.

Birth control was practiced in all of the native cultures around the world that Weston Price studied. By tribal custom, they spaced

Opposite: A woman of the Pomo Nation sifts flour in a wide basket. Prior to contact with whites, the flour would most likely have been corn. After settlement on reservations, Indians were taught to farm with the tools used by whites and to raise the few crops brought from Europe, including wheat.

their children at least three years apart. Among the highly mobile Lakota, ideal spacing was five years. This was seen as being beneficial to both children and mothers. It was assumed that to grow strong and secure, all children needed undivided attention from an unstressed mother for the first several years of their lives.

Dr. Price interviewed a physician who was head of a hospital of Canada's largest Indian reservation, in Ontario. According to the doctor, while the grandmothers of the current generation of Indian women gave birth without difficulty at home, current mothers went into the hospital and were in labor for days, sometimes requiring surgery. Needless to say, the grandmothers had been eating the diet of their female ancestors, while their granddaughters' diets contained refined foods.

In observing precontact skeletons unearthed in southern Florida, Dr. Price found no influence of arthritis in the joints, while modern Indians in the area had both rheumatoid arthritis and tooth decay. The active life of native people combined with their diet kept them strong and healthy, physically and spiritually.

THE GOOD LIFE

Reports given directly by whites who lived with hunter-gatherer Indians confirms Dr. Price's findings. They recounted that the daily work hours were shorter and the time for recreation and human enjoyment longer than that of the European settlers. Benjamin Franklin worried that while Indian children taken by whites returned to their people as soon as possible if given the opportunity, when the situation was reversed and white children were taken to live with Indian tribes, there was not one case of a child volunteering to return to white society. Sometimes when people attempted to reclaim children who had adapted at a young age to Indian life on the frontier, they had to be taken by force.

Some anthropologists have termed hunter-gatherers the original affluent societies. It might easily be assumed that some of the bad feeling toward Indians on the part of early white settlers stemmed from jealousy aroused by the sight of a people who lived, in many respects, just like the aristocrats of Europe that the settlers had hoped to leave behind. The Indian men went off hunting and fishing, while the white peasants endlessly tilled the soil. There are accounts of early white men describing Indian men who, having successfully completed a strenuous hunt and returned to camp to relax, were waited upon by women grateful for the meat and hides, and lay about, telling jokes and enjoying themselves shamelessly.

Life for native women, while more consistently active than that of some of the men, was still comparatively easy. While native women spent quite some time at their farming, they never planted more than they needed for family or clan. The women usually worked together in groups, singing as they went, and then rested together in the shade of a tree.

The enjoyment of daily life of Indian women is attested to by Mary Jemison, a white woman, who was fifteen when taken by the Seneca to replace the relative of an Indian family killed in battle. Hers is one of the best known and important white "captivity" stories, which grew in popularity in the eighteenth and early nineteenth centuries as the settlers pushed west and the struggle between native nations and the whites intensified. Often the former captives returning to white society were encouraged to amend their stories to reflect badly on their former captors. Mary Jemison's story is important for the fact that she did not do this, living as she did for the rest of her life among the Seneca, finally telling her story when she was eighty years old.

In Mary's estimation, Indian women certainly worked no harder than white women, and probably enjoyed life more. "We planted, tended, and harvested our corn, and generally had all our children with us; but had no master to oversee or drive us, so that we could work as leisurely as we pleased."

In white farming communities, people did not work as cooperatively as they did in hunter-gatherer or early agricultural societies such as those of the native peoples of North America. While white families worked together on barn raisings or bringing in the harvest, and the women got together to work on their sewing, much of the time the family farm operated as a self-contained unit. This put a premium on having as many children as possible, which placed a terrible burden on women. In pioneer days, it was typical for a man to bury at least one if not two or more wives in the quest for little farm workers. To defend their difficult way of life, Europeans made a god of "hard work" that endures to this day as the "work ethic." Anyone not possessing this ethic, anyone seen to enjoy his or her life too much, is viewed with envy and suspicion, even today.

GERM WARFARE AND THE EUROPEAN INVASION

According to both oral history and the archaeological record, native people of both North and South America were remarkably free of diseases such as smallpox and the black plague that ravaged the European populations at the time of the conquest.

While the precise reasons for this may never be fully known, it is true that native people as a whole valued cleanliness and bathed often. Luther Standing Bear (Lakota), writes of the early morning bath as part of the ritual of greeting the day. Native peoples used various materials with which to clean themselves, including the yucca plant. By contrast, at the time that the Spanish invaded South America, most whites abhorred bathing. Rampant disease in Europe was only contained with the advent of soap and its liberal application. These facts lead to the interesting point that the main killer of Indians during the conquest—and what many historians consider to have been responsible for the success of the European invasion—was not superior weaponry, but germ warfare.

At the time of the Spanish invasion, a European marksman could load and fire but one shot while a well-trained Indian marksman could get off ten arrows. However, Europeans brought with them a plague of devastating diseases which spread like wildfire across the continent as one Indian tribe traded with another. Many of the Indians who died from these diseases never saw the white men who brought them. Afflictions like smallpox were so deadly and spread so fast that Indian medicine people did not have time to develop cures before the dreadful scourges did their work.

Below: Arapaho women have their skinning knives out, preparing to process the kill. This photograph was probably taken on the Wind River Reservation in Wyoming after 1878.

In a very evil chapter in white-red relations, European invaders recognized this weakness of the Indians, and exploited it on more than one occasion by giving germ-infected blankets as gifts to the cold and unsuspecting. Thus was born modern germ warfare.

FEEDING FROM THE MOTHER

Dale Carson, an Abenaki who lives in Connecticut, is both a craftswoman and a wonderful cook. In her *New Native American Cooking*, Ms. Carson offers over one hundred mouth-watering examples of how the foods and cooking traditions of native people can be updated for modern enjoyment and health.

At a recent event where Ms. Carson was asked to serve a large gathering, she discovered that the thirty pounds of buffalo meat required for the entire group rendered but one-half of a cup of fat! Today, physicians often prescribe buffalo meat to their heart patients and others who must control their cholesterol. Buffalo, now raised by ranchers, is also free of steroids and pesticides.

Traditional Indian cooking was simple. When food comes fresh from a garden or picked from the vine at just the right moment, its delicious taste need not be hidden by artificial flavorings or masked by sharp spices. A favorite and very simple desert of Dale Carson's is wild rice served cold under a thick drizzle of real maple syrup. As Dale says, "Scarcely anyone believes that just two humble ingredients create such elegant flavor."

Among the coastal peoples, fish was, of course, a staple of the diet. Fish was often caught in weirs. In Boston harbor, a 4,500-year old fish weir was discovered in the 1920s that covered more than two acres under water, pointing to the existence of a very sizeable Indian community.

Before overfishing depleted the fish population, fish was extremely plentiful in harbors and lakes. Along the coasts, shell fish, crab and lobster were steamed in pits by people who came to down to the shore to live in summer camps and then move back inland to winter camps for the hunting of deer and other wild game.

There is no known instance of the domestication of farm animals among the native people of North America, such as was done in Europe. Native people did not use dairy products until the post-contact period.

When discussing Indian cooking, it is hard not to recall the story of how the Indians saved the early Pilgrims from starvation by feeding them. The story points up a number of interesting truths. When Europeans first arrived on the continent, they did not understand the country and did not know its wild plants and animals

Left: A cache of salmon is stored in a convenient tree by Salish people in this photograph taken on the Fraser River, Lytton, British Columbia. Fish was carefully dried before storage.

and their proper uses. At the time of contact, native people were using more than one thousand different plants for food, at least one hundred of which they had cultivated themselves. The Europeans would literally have starved to death without Indian generosity. Among indigenous people who live very close to Earth and her moods and seasons, generosity and hospitality are of necessity among the primary virtues.

An example of how Indians view generosity may be seen in the potlatches or "giveaways" practiced by the peoples of the Northwest. Giveaways were an integral part of the life of most Indian nations, although practiced in different forms. The potlatches were ceremonies in which a family would give away all of its possessions, usually to the needier members of the tribe. This would be done to celebrate a birth, a death, to commemorate some strong event in the life of a family. Because possessions may be easily enough regained by those who are capable, and because no tribe would let

a member go hungry or in want, the giveaway did not endanger the family but rather showed its ability to acquire things and then have the strength and generosity to give them all away again. White missionaries from a capitalistic, acquisitive society viewed this practice with such horror that potlatches were made illegal for a time, along with other Indian rites and ceremonials, like the Sun Dance of the Plains Indians.

While corn, beans and squash were long cultivated, Indians across the continent gathered much of their food from the wild, including berries, wild rice and roots. Especially in warmer months, food was fresh and plentiful. Women, who collected these supplies, were so attuned to nature that they knew for example that some berries tasted better when the pickers stood downwind of the bush.

Across the continent, most native women spent a good deal of time drying the meat or fish that the men caught. Drying meat requires that it be as fresh as possible to begin with, and then sliced very thin so that it can dry quickly before it can spoil. Wooden drying racks were erected around the tipi, earth lodge or hogan. It was often dried over a low, smoky fire, which helped keep the flies away. Once dry, the meat could be stored for years. It was often stored in parfleches, satchels made of leather, which could travel with a hunting family, or be stored underground in a secret

Below: This photo shows a Zuni woman using the old corn grinding method. Grinding all of the corn required for her family was a daily task for women of the Southwest. Many traditional Navajo, Hopi and other Pueblo women still grind corn by hand.

cache. Among the Plains people, stew was a favorite dish, eaten for breakfast, lunch or dinner. The dried meat was boiled for hours until tender, and vegetables were added.

While Indian women traditionally cooked their soups, chowders and stews in everything from watertight baskets to buffalo stomachs, in the postcontact period, iron pots quickly replaced these items. Soups were the mainstay of many indigenous peoples, as they could be started early in the day and added to as the ingredients were gathered. Many villages had communal pots from which everyone was welcome to eat.

Indian fried bread is considered part of a "traditional" Indian meal and is a favorite at powwows today, where it is a special treat when covered with honey. It is also served with stew. The simple ingredients include flour, baking powder, salt and water. While yeast was introduced by the Europeans, Indians, like other peoples around the world, baked bread from time immemorial, the ingredients coming from cornmeal, berries, acorns, cattails, amaranth, hazelnuts, reedgrass, yams, squash, sunflower and other wild grains and nuts. In the Southwest, bread was more commonly baked in the form of tortillas.

Indian berry soup was used much like a modern pudding, a healthy dessert as well as a treat and a sacred meal for events such

Below: *This 1939 photograph was taken on the Navajo Reservation. Native women traditionally ground corn by hand, but community corn grinders such as this one were set up for faster results.*

Above: *Hopi women are shown baking bread in one of the beehive-shaped ovens still used by traditional native women across the southwest.*

as medicine pipe ceremonies. The berries were picked and dried in the sun for several days. When used, they had first to be soaked until tender. The soaked berries were then mixed with a meat broth and thickened with flour.

CORN, A SACRED FOOD

Of the foods developed by native women, corn achieved the highest, almost a mythic, status among the native nations of the Americas. It was certainly considered the staff of life.

Pueblo people celebrate corn as coming from the Corn Mothers, Blue Corn Woman and White Corn Maiden, who brought the precious food with them when they climbed through the kiva roof onto the surface of the earth. Corn plays a ritual part in the life of a child from its birth, when the infant receives an ear of corn made into a fetish, which it keeps for life.

While Pueblo men work the fields, still, the fields belong to the women, as do the sacred objects of the clan. It is through the female line that Pueblos trace their descent. While Pueblo women do not cultivate their corn like their Seneca sisters to the north, they are

expert at grinding it by hand, using grinding stones passed down from their mothers. The women also build and repair their apartmentlike homes, which they also own.

As Dale Carson writes in *New Native American Cooking*, "Popcorn is among the foods most identified with Native Americans. The corn itself was cultivated widely by the Inca civilization and is known to have been farmed far into the northern cultural regions. Legend has it that the 'popping' feature was discovered quite by accident when kernels carelessly dropped in the hot coals of a cooking fire started a culinary explosion. Although it's not clear how ancient the art of popping really is, English documents describe how (Wampanoag leader) Massasoit's brother Quadequina brought a bushel of popped corn to a thanksgiving dinner held in 1621."

Many rituals grew up around this important crop. Many tribes of the Southeast hold the Green Corn ceremony, or the Busk, held at the end of each summer's corn harvest. This ritual of thanksgiving and renewal came down from ancient times. People cleaned their houses and made good their relationships. Village elders and medicine people fasted and purified themselves. During the ritual, the high priest ceremonially lit the new sacred fire, which was carried in the dance. When the dance was over, home fires were relit with the new sacred fire and the women prepared the thanksgiving feast. The ancient ritual was completed as the villagers purified themselves in a nearby stream. The people were ready for the new year to begin.

Below: This photograph depicts women cooking before a tipi while corn dries on racks in the foreground. Native women across the continent grew corn. Even the mobile Plains Indians planted the crop in the spring and came to harvest it when it was grown.

LIVING ARTS AND SKILLS

Our life is our art.

> —JEAN LAMARR, PAIUTE-PITT RIVER ARTIST,
> UNIVERSITY PROFESSOR

The dance is like a conduit through which the energies of nature may be channeled in order to obtain a balance between Earth and Sky. The drum is like the heartbeat of the earth. Experiencing the dance transports both the dancer and the observer.

> —M. K. KEEGAN, EUROPEAN AUTHOR

Opposite: Navajo weavers, circa 1895. Traditional Navajo weavers still perform all stages of the craft by hand, from raising sheep to dying wool to designing the finished product.

In keeping with their holistic view of life, Indian women did not distinguish between "art" and the decorations with which they graced everyday objects, be these objects sacred or mundane. Before the coming of the white man, Indians did not have prisons; neither did they have museums. In the vast majority of cultures, finely crafted objects were not the purview of the wealthy, but were enjoyed by all. In *We're Still Here*, Suzanne Fox writes about the meaning in the natural objects she uses in her jewelry. "The spirits of the plants and animals are still there. When we wear them, they become part of us."

Today, the best of all types of Indian art, including hand-dyed and -woven Navajo blankets, pottery and paintings, command top prices and are in demand around the world. But before the tourist, cavalry officer and fur trader, native women were putting part of their souls into the decoration of clothing, tipis, jewelry, pots and baskets for spiritual as well as aesthetic reasons.

Among native people, dishes were a democratic utensil. One set of pottery was made and used by the family. There was no parallel to today's kitchen in which there are several sets of dishes, with fine china used only for "best." Hungry strangers coming to an Indian home ate from the same dish as everyone else. When people gather in a circle to eat, there is no place "below the salt."

In Indian life across the continent, women made most of the family belongings, from the house itself to the clothes, pots, baskets, ceremonial objects, mats, pillows, rugs, ropes and gardening tools. Few of these items were made without a touch of grace that marked the artist as an individual creator, as well as one who was continuing the traditions of her people.

73

While women did the cooking and made most of the clothing, men had to have some knowledge of these arts in order to survive during hunting season when they were away from camp. Men were also responsible for making their own implements used for hunting and war. Among the Plains people, it was the men who made the famous pictographs, lifelike drawings done on hides, that told the stories of their prowess in war and on the hunt. They might paint these on the outside of their tipis for all to see.

By tradition, women of the Plains Indian tribes used only geometric designs in their work, circles and triangles arranged in patterns. A woman of the Blood nation might decorate her tipi using stylized motifs that were handed down through generations of the women of her family.

HOME

Below: This turn-of-the-century photograph shows the interior of an adobe dwelling.

With a sense of art and great craft, women made almost everything that went into the home, including the home itself. At the time of European contact, depending upon the nation and its location, the clan or family home came in a variety of styles, including the skin tipi of the Plains culture, the earth lodge of the Mandans, the apartment house of the southwestern Pueblos, the log hogans

of the Navajo, the bark covered longhouse of the northeastern Iroquois and the porchlike home of the southeastern Seminole.

All of these styles had in common the fact that their materials came from the surrounding habitat and were designed to work within the natural environment. To remain cool in summer, a Navajo family moved to its summer hogan, which was constructed so that breezes could blow through. On the plains, the bottom of the skirt of a tipi could be rolled up for the same purpose. The Seminole "chickee" was an open porch, a raised platform with no sides. Earth lodges such as those of the Mandans naturally kept inhabitants cool in summer and warm in winter.

Pueblo men erected the walls and roof beams, but the women plastered pueblo walls and covered the roof with grass, brushwood and mud. To build a tipi, Plains women would gather in a group, much like a European sewing circle, and under the direction of a head woman skilled in the art, stitch together the six to eight buffalo hides required. The size of the tipi varied depending upon the size of the family it would house. The stretching, scraping and tanning that went into the preparation of the hides prior to sewing could take days.

Many homes, like tipis and longhouses, could be taken down and moved fairly easily. Entire Iroquois towns consisting of a thousand inhabitants could remove to a different location, giving rest to cultivated lands. When the Seminole moved camp, one clan was required by tradition to remove all signs of human occupa-

Above: An Arizona woman of an unknown tribe uses branches to fashion the foundation of a simple dwelling. It is probably a wickiup, a hut traditionally finished with a covering of mats.

Above: *A Sauk and Fox woman stands in front of her lodge. Such dwellings, which were covered with heavy reed mats, were known throughout the northeast.*

tion. In hunting cultures like the Plains people, when necessary, a camp could be on the move in less than half an hour, tipis down and gear packed on the travois.

Luther Standing Bear (Lakota) writes of the idyllic home life of his Plains Indian childhood in which his mother played a central role:

"Though the leaders of the tribe selected the site for the village, the woman of the household selected the place…for her tipi…[and] put it up herself. If the tipi were very large she might need assistance, but the help of a man would not be welcomed. There were always plenty of other women about…As soon as the tipi was put up, a fire was built. Clean grass was gathered and spread on the floor and over this rugs of rawhide were thrown. These rugs were stiff and kept their place on the floor, and with the hair side up were pleasant to live on. They were easily lifted up and not infrequently taken outside to be dusted and cleaned. The furnishings of the tipi home were all the handiwork of the women. They tanned and sewed together the skins of the tipi, made floor rugs suitable in size, filled soft buckskin pillows with cottonwood floss and finished the blankets spread over the tripod bed. Painted bags and clothes containers decorated with brightly hued quillwork hung against the brown walls of the Indian woman's home….No home,

whatever the material used in construction, is cleaner, more sanitary or livable-in than a freshly erected tipi. And no home, dimly lit with shaded lamps, is more cheerful than a tipi home lit by the flickering glow of a cedar fire."

CLOTHING

Indian women made nearly all of the clothing that their families wore. Men learned to make basic repairs to clothing just as they learned basic cooking, in order to survive on the hunt or at war, whenever women did not accompany them.

When Europeans first arrived, typical dress for New England Indians was similar to that of many of the northern and Plains tribes. The man wore a breechcloth, which was a long piece of skin drawn between the legs and tucked under a belt; skin leggings were attached to the belt with thongs and held in place by garters wrapped at the knee. Belts and garters were of leather or woven plant fibers.

Left: Dressed in a beaded gown and exquisite headdress, a young Wisham woman of the Pacific Northwest has had her nose pierced with the traditional sliver of bone and tiny ring. Piercing of the ears, nose and lower lip were also favored by the Yupik women of southern Alaska.

Right: A Lakota mother carries her baby in a skillfully decorated cradle board.

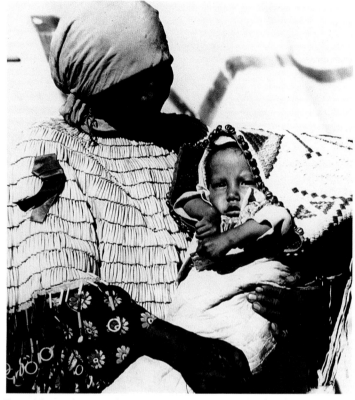

In cold weather, a robe was worn over one shoulder, the exposed arm protected by an animal pelt.

Before European contact, Plains Indians wore buffalo robes as cloaks. After contact, especially with the destruction of the buffalo, their robes were replaced by the wool blankets given out by the government or obtained in trade. Among Plains Indians, the blanket, or robe, was a method of communication when noise and shouting might scare away the game. From a hill top, a scout could signal with his blanket to inform the hunters in camp if he had found game in the area and where the game was located. As described by Luther Standing Bear, a young Lakota interested in wooing a lady would wrap himself up in his best blanket before setting out. If extremely shy, he might leave only one eye exposed, forcing the object of his desires to guess at first just who this male admirer might be. If things went well, it was proper for him to put his blanket across her shoulders as they walked together. Today, when Plains Indians marry in the traditional manner, they stand together under the blanket. Giving up city life for the reservation and the traditional manner of living still conducted by many native elders is referred to as "going back to the blanket."

Human beings universally take pride in their appearance, none more so than the Plains Indians. While usually stripped down for battle, each warrior adorned himself carefully with body paint and feathers before heading out for serious business. Any clothing that was worn into battle was of the best. Today, Alex White Plume, (Oglala Lakota) of the Pine Ridge Reservation, is frequently asked to consult on film productions whose directors concern themselves with historical authenticity. At a recent visit to a set on which he was not consulting, Mr. White Plume took one look at the Indian warrior actors and announced, "All Lakota women are going to be embarrassed when this movie comes out, based on the clothing. We would look good when we went into battle. [This clothing] makes them look like skid row bums…!"

Among the northern tribes, women also wore the breechcloth, leggings shorter than the men's and wraparound skirts that folded over a belt. Their robes were longer than a man's would be and were composed of several skins. After European contact, woolen shawls replaced animal hide robes. Today, shawls are considered proper wear for women when attending formal ceremonies.

Below: Navajo women weavers continue to color their wools with dyes made from native plants. Here, an elder woman twists the dyed wool into yarn with the use of a spindle.

Above: These Arapaho women of the Wind River Indian Reservation in Wyoming have staked an animal hide to process it. After they have scraped the hide to remove all fat and excess hair, they will cure it with animal brains and leave it in the sun to complete the tanning process.

Both women and men wore the soft-soled moccasins used by Indian nations across the continent. They carried pouches of leather or woven fiber. Precontact clothing was decorated with moose hair or porcupine quill embroidery and had painted designs made from bright natural dyes that came from plants. While little remains of the original clothing, historians believe that these early garments were richly decorated (see section on quillwork below). Native women spent a great deal of time and care creating garments that were beautiful as well as practical.

Leather clothing was sewn using an awl and animal sinews, of different thicknesses depending upon their use, and these implements were stored in kits. When a young woman proved her worth at sewing, she was proud to wear one of these kits at her belt, which proclaimed her a capable adult woman. This was her counterpart to the activity of the young man who had to prove himself through a successful hunt.

Obtaining leather required several steps—first, catching the animal appropriate for the intended use. Then followed skinning it properly and tanning the hide, which required several more steps: stretching, scraping, brushing, cleaning, oiling, curing and drying. Deer skin, thin and light but still strong, was preferred for clothing. The heavier hides of buffalo, moose and elk were used for tipi covers, robes and moccasins. Plains winter moccasins, head cov-

erings and mittens were made from buffalo hide with the fur left on and worn inside. Warm buffalo robes were slept in on cold prairie nights.

Many leather clothing items were fringed, which had a practical as well as an aesthetic use. They acted as wicks to draw water away from the body of a leather garment, allowing it to dry quickly. For a people who lived out-of-doors, keeping dry was serious business.

When the Europeans arrived, bringing their own goods and styles, Indian women integrated the new elements into their clothing designs. As game became more scarce, they used trade cloth instead of skins when making the traditional wrapped and folded clothing: leggings, skirts, breechcloths and the like. Cloth was not as durable as leather and harder to care for. However, it was easier to obtain and cooler in summer.

CROSSING CULTURES

Even in prehistoric times, people moved about a great deal, interacting with each other and trading as they went. Designs and materials found their way across the continent through visits and intermarriage. While unique designs and artifacts are to be found in different locations (like the distinctive pottery designs of the Pueblo) there are many more similarities. While their specific designs may vary, baskets, for example, are to be found in all parts of the North American continent as well as in Central America.

When the whites came to live among them, native people "indianized" non-native technology, adapting materials to suit their

Left: This collection includes from left to right a Nez Perce corn husking bag, circa 1910, a Paiute wedding basket and a piece of pottery from the Acoma Pueblo, displayed on a Navajo blanket. Even during prehistoric times, people moved around, intermarrying, trading, exchanging ideas and art forms. While some designs and art forms are unique to specific locations, evidence of this type of exchange is apparent.

81

needs. Glass beads are a prime example. Easier than porcupine quills for use as decoration, beads became highly prized and were used in trade for furs. Today among Indian bead workers, crystal from Czechoslovakia is considered to have the highest quality. Native people also came to use acrylic wool for finger weaving, and glass jars as molds for basketry vases.

In the late nineteenth century, pushed onto reservations and in need of new ways to feed their families, many Indians began to create works of art specifically designed to be sold to tourists. This required understanding the market, what the buyers would respond to and what to charge. While the need to appeal to tourists certainly affected Indian art, it also helped keep traditions alive. Like the communities themselves, although affected by the outer world, the art of Indian people remains traditional at its very core. Splint fancy baskets are a good example of traditional Indian work that has changed to suit the needs of a white audience. Traditional splint basketry, once beautiful but utilitarian, was given added decoration to appeal to ornate Victorian tastes.

Silk ribbons, originally from Europe, became popular for use as decorations for clothing. The ribbon shirt originated among the Plains tribes, where native women added interest to simple calico shirts by sewing strips of silk ribbons across front and back, leaving long strips free to move gracefully like grass in the wind when the wearer walked or danced. Ribbons also recalled the traditional leather fringes.

By the mid-nineteenth century in New England, and by the late-nineteenth century farther to the west, Indians began dressing in European clothing, wearing Indian traditional dress only for formal occasions. Today, native people refer to Indian dress as "regalia" and wear it when they wish to identify their Indian culture, at powwows and other ceremonial gatherings.

While native women were quick to integrate European forms and materials into their clothing repertoire, their traditional designs have in turn influenced white society. The leather fringe is a classic decoration of leather jackets. During the late 1960s, the beads, flowers and head bands of American youth were based on the traditional designs of native women. Bead work and stitched-thread designs on shirts and blue jeans become popular in the 1970s and 1980s, especially as jeans became the uniform of youth the world over. In a 1995 *New York Times* article, young people from several cultures were shown with their hair in long braids wrapped in the Indian braid ties made popular by American Indian Movement activists.

More practical examples of the way Indian women's ingenuity has affected society include the parka, which was invented by Eskimo. American and European women are discovering the practicality and healthful nature of the cradle board. This mode of baby transport supports soft, still-forming limbs while allowing baby to remain close to mother as she goes through her day. In some German hospitals, new babies are sent home in cradle boards. As one Navajo mother phrased it, "The whites are learning."

POTTERY

The earliest pots discovered in North America by archaeologists were found in the present-day state of Georgia, and date back to 2,500 BC. They were simple vessels with organic fibers mixed into the clay to keep them from cracking when fired. At these sites, archaeologists found no trace of agriculture, so presumably pottery was made and used by hunter-gatherer peoples.

Left: Hopi woman making pottery. Photograph by Charles Carpenter, 1901. According to archaeologists, pottery existed during the pre-agricultural, hunter-gatherer era. In North America, the earliest pots discovered, in Georgia, date back to 2500 BC.

Above: These fine examples of modern Hopi pottery were crafted by artisans in Arizona.

Today, when we think of Indian pottery, it is likely that our first image will be of the Southwest. Southwest artists have developed this very traditional and practical craft to such a high level that many collectors consider it unsurpassed. The wealthy from around the world come to Santa Fe each year and spend thousands of dollars collecting it. Museums covet the finest pieces.

Collectors consider the legendary Maria Montoya Martinez of San Ildefonso Pueblo to be one of the greatest of the potters, although there are many. With the help of her husband, Marie—as she often signed her work—revived the ancient Pueblo craft of pottery-making and encouraged interest in Pueblo pottery among both whites and Indians. The pottery revival helped restore the economy of San Ildefonso. As other native women would do with other native forms, Marie revived a traditional art, preserving it while taking it to a new level, as with the beautiful black-on-black pottery that she developed. Among many honors, Marie received the medal of the American Institute of Architects and the French Palmes Academiques.

Back in the early 1930s, when Maria began selling her work, a more elaborate piece might go for as much as fifty dollars. Today, that very pot would fetch two hundred thousand. Maria's dream was to revive a beautiful art form and pass it to the next generations, and in this she succeeded. When she died in 1980, she left twenty-four great-grandchildren, many of whom continue the tradition.

While southwest pottery is known around the world, Indian people made and used clay pots in most parts of the continent. In

the Northeast, the Wampanoag Indian people of Gay Head on Martha's Vineyard gathered multi-colored clays from the island cliffs to make their distinctive cooking pots and storage jars. When white tourists began arriving on the island, the Wampanoags made their pots to sell. To preserve the lively color of the clays, the Wampanoags did not fire their pots, but baked them in the sun.

BASKETRY

In some places, the soil does not contain good clay for pots. Native women became adept at making baskets that served in the place of pots, including pots for cooking. This was accomplished by heating stones and dropping them into water-filled baskets that had been sealed tight with clay. Plains Indians used buffalo innards as cooking pots in much the same way.

Basketry has a long tradition in the Northeast. Women used splints from the ash or basket tree to weave large baskets, used to store dried foods, gather wild foods, harvest and transport crops. By the mid-eighteenth century, northeastern Indians were selling such baskets to their European neighbors. It was once thought

Below: These Navajo baskets display the remarkable color, design and texture of the native handiwork. Women across the continent made baskets for many uses. Large baskets enabled women to carry heavy loads with the aid of a strap across the forehead. Tightly woven baskets were used to carry water.

that the Shakers invented this craft, but apparently they learned it from the Passamaquoddy of Maine. Basket weaving is a tradition that continues in New England today. In southern New England, basket weavers stamped or painted splints with floral and plant designs. In Maine, they created designs by coloring the entire splint.

Wooden blocks of different shapes and sizes were used to "block" the various baskets. As with songs and stories, the women passed their basket blocks on to their daughters and their granddaughters, one generation passing the traditions to the next.

QUILLWORK AND BEADWORK

Lakota elder Alice New Holy Blue Legs is considered one of the best quillworkers in the world today. She has received numerous awards including a National Endowment for the Arts Award in 1985. Her quillwork is on display at the Smithsonian Institution in Washington, D.C. She has passed the now-rare knowledge of the art of quillwork to her daughters and granddaughters.

Above: A woman of the Chippewa nation demonstrates her craft at the Louisiana Purchase Exposition in St. Louis, Missouri. Photograph by Charles Carpenter, 1904.

Opposite: A Ruby Creek Salish woman weaves and braids rushes to form a superbly shaped basket. Photograph taken at Ruby Creek, Lower Fraser River, British Columbia.

Above: *These items display the intricate detail in beading and quilling that goes into the creation of even the smallest items. Few surfaces were left unadorned in some fashion.*

Alice is keeping alive a tradition that is ancient among her people. Ten years ago in the Black Hills of South Dakota, where caves run deep in the cold earth, archaeologists discovered the well-preserved body of a young woman whose buckskin dress was still intact. Scientists dated the find at approximately 1,000 BC. The ancient dress was decorated in quillwork that could have been done by Alice.

The difficulty involved in this beautiful craft may immediately be grasped when one considers that, if written as a recipe, the first instruction might be "catch a porcupine." Quills that were used for sewing decorations had to be chewed by the artist to soften and flatten them, a time-consuming task. Quillworkers today still soak the quills in their mouths to make them soft and pliant and then flatten them with their teeth. When sewn onto an article of clothing, quills somewhat resemble dried grass, but are very durable, as the archaeological find attests.

Initially, quills were dyed with berries or bark. After being forced onto reservations, women obtained dye more easily by extracting the blues and reds from government blankets that were cut into strips and boiled. Porcupine quills were also left in their naturally attractive shades of brown and tan. Quills used as jewelry, like earrings or necklaces, are left in their natural rounded state.

With the advent of the Europeans, beads could be obtained in trade. Many women turned to this method of decoration, which was quicker and easier than quilling, one reason why there are so few quillworkers left today. Of all the many Indian crafts, bead work is today the most popular form.

Old-fashioned seed beads, made in Italy, had colors that were soft and uneven in shape, which gave the finished work an uneven "hand" or surface texture. As mentioned above, Czechoslovakian beads, preferred by today's crafts people, are considered to have the highest quality. Their colors and bright and clear, and they come in regular even sizes which give modern finished work a distinctively smooth feel to the hand.

Left: Wisham bride, photographed by Edward S. Curtis. This young woman's dress is covered with decorations, most but not all of which could be obtained locally. Most of the beads are probably of sea shell, easily gathered in the northwest coastal area. The bones that form the choker around her neck would have come from indigenous animals, as would porcupine quills for any quillwork. Glass beads would come from Europe. The coins on her headdress probably came from Asia through trade.

NAVAJO WEAVERS

Navajo rug makers weave their magic by hand using age-old methods that cannot be improved upon by modern technology.

Members of the Ramah Navajo Weavers Association, a cooperative of forty members spanning five generations, view their art as a prayer and their craft as a way of life. Rug making begins with caring for the soils that their flocks graze upon, and breeding those flocks to improve the quality of the wool. The wool from churro sheep, a rare breed considered the ancestral sheep of the People, have long, coarse fibers ideally suited for hand carding and spinning, and come in several earth tones as well as ebony and black. Churro wool contains less lanolin than other breeds, making it easier to dye by hand using wild plants. Wild plants, considered gifts from the spirit people, are treated with reverence. The women never take more than are needed for the project at hand.

For color, the herb called Navajo tea is used when a weaver wants to dye newly spun wool a golden earth tone. Herb madder is used to produce peach colors; dried cactus bugs give deep reds; ripe cactus fruit produces pinks; walnut shells give browns; juniper berries, snakeweed and wild carrot create bright yellows; and for blues, the indigo plant is employed. Dye pots are carefully tended over outdoor fires. It takes twenty days to prepare yarn, and thirty to forty days to complete an average thirty-by-sixty-inch weaving.

Below: Navajo exhibit their blankets in Bluff, Utah, at the turn of the century.

At one time, going through non-Indian middlemen, the Ramah women were able to obtain only one-fifth of the value of their creations. Coop members are now able to market their own wares, and have received awards for their creations. With handmade beauty and designs that reflect Navajo spiritual values of balance and harmony, Navajo weavings appeal to people the world over.

SONGS AND STORIES

Songs and storytelling were always part of life for native people. Songs were created and sung and danced to celebrate every major event in the life of a person, a family or a nation. Russell Means (Lakota) has said, "We have a song for everything. Name something. We have a song for it.…Each ingredient of the dance has a relationship to the others and together they keep the vision alive. It's that relationship that makes the culture."

Among most nations, especially the Iroquois, oratory was raised to a very high art. At the great council meetings of the Six Nations, the best speakers could hold an audience spellbound for hours at a time. On several occasions, visiting Europeans made note of this fact in their journals and letters.

As far as is known, Indian nations of the North American continent did not have systems of writing until the advent of the Europeans. Thus, clan stories and songs were passed orally from one generation to the next. The oral tradition develops in young people a very keen ability to remember, very accurately, what they hear. This tradition lives today among tribal council members of the Nez Perce who can, without reference to notes, recall verbatim the debates in council that may have taken place decades before. Their accuracy can be checked against written notes taken at the time by the council secretary.

Because songs and stories were not written down, many were lost during the great holocaust of the European invasion. However, beginning in the late nineteenth century, Indian women and men began to commit stories to paper, and a unique style of written literature was born. Native American literature—in written form—is now a growing art whose practitioners are becoming recognized on the international scene.

One of the main themes of native literature is the struggle of the mixed-blood Indian to find his or her place in the modern world. Indian literature is often expressed in an episodic manner as opposed to the linear beginning-middle-end style of western tradition. Great native writers, like the brilliant Louise Erdrich (Chippewa, German-American), often draw upon the myths and legends of their heritage while at the same time exploring universal human truths. In her moving novel *Ceremony*, MacArthur Foundation Grantee Leslie Marmon Silko (Laguna Pueblo, Mexican, European) uses another popular theme, the return of the war veteran and his struggle to re-enter reservation life.

Through subtle humor with a very keen edge, native writers also make original and perceptive observations of mainstream American life. Their unique dual position as insiders-outsiders gives them an important vantage point from which to view and report on the passing scene.

Emily Pauline Johnson, (Canadian Mohawk, 1861–1913), achieved critical acclaim as a poet and a performer of her work in Canada, the United States and England. Ella Deloria (Lakota, 1888–1971) wrote movingly about life on the plains in her novel, *Waterlily*, in which the action centers around the lives of the women, unusual for its time.

Below: Tipi of Strikes on Both Sides, Blackfoot Nation. Photograph by Walter McClintock. This interior view shows the care and skill required to create a warm and comfortable Plains dwelling. Parfleches could be stored behind the decorated hanging lining the walls, which also retains heat.

The following is a sample of Native American literature from the final page of chapter one of Louise Erdrich's national best-selling novel, *Love Medicine*:

Even when it started to snow she did not lose her sense of direction. Her feet grew numb, but she did not worry about the distance. The heavy winds couldn't blow her off course. She continued. Even when her heart clenched and her skin turned crackling cold it didn't matter, because the pure and naked part of her went on.

The snow fell deeper that Easter than it had in forty years, but June walked over it like water and came home.

BIBLIOGRAPHY

Allen, Paula Gunn, ed. *Spider Woman's Granddaughters, Traditional Tales and Contemporary Writing by Native American Women.* Ballantine Books, 1989.

—— *Voice of the Turtle, American Indian Literature, 1900–1970.* Ballantine Books, 1994.

—— *The Sacred Hoop, Recovering the Feminine in American Indian Traditions.* Beacon Press, 1992.

Ballentine, Betty and Ian, ed. *The Native Americans, An Illustrated History.* Turner Publishing, Inc., 1993.

Bataille, Gretchen M. and Sands, Kathleen Mullen. *American Indian Women, Telling Their Lives.* University of Nebraska Press, 1984.

Brave Bird, Mary. *Ohitika Woman.* Harper-Perennial, 1994.

Brown, Dee. *Bury My Heart at Wounded Knee, An Indian History of the American West.* Henry Holt and Company, New York, 1991.

Carson, Dale. *Native New England Cooking.* Peregrine Press, Connecticut. 1980.

Churchill, Ward. *Fantasies of the Master Race, Literature, Cinema and the Colonization of American Indians.* Common Courage Press, 1992.

Crow Dog, Mary. *Lakota Woman.* Harper-Perennial, 1990.

Deloria, Ella C. *Waterlily.* University of Nebraska Press, 1988.

Deloria, Jr., Vine. *Custer Died For Your Sins.* University of Oklahoma Press, 1988.

Dockstader, Frederick J. *Indian Art of the Americas.* New York Museum of the American Indian, Heye Foundation, 1973.

Douglas, Frederic H., and D'Harnoncourt, Rene. *Indian Art of the United States.* The Museum of Modern Art, New York, 1941.

Erdoes, Richard. *Crying for a Dream: The World Through Native American Eyes.* Bear & Company Publishing, 1989.

Erdrich, Louise. *Love Medicine.* Holt, Rinehart & Winston, New York, 1984.

Farley, Ronnie. *Women of the Native Struggle.* Orion Books, New York, 1993.

Feder, Norman. *American Indian Art.* Harry N. Abrams, Inc., New York, 1966.

Green, Rayna. *Women in American Indian Society.* Chelsea House Publishers, 1992.

Gridley, Marion E. *American Indian Women.* Hawthorn Books, Inc., New York, 1974.

Heth, Carlotte, ed. *Native American Dance: Ceremonies and Social Traditions.* National Museum of the American Indian, Washington, D.C., 1992.

Hirschfelder, Arlene, ed. *Native Heritage, Personal Accounts by American Indians 1790 to the Present.* MacMillan, 1995.

Hothem, Lar. *North American Indian Artifacts.* Books Americana Inc., Florence, Alabama, 1978.

Hungry Wolf, Beverly. *The Ways of My Grand-mothers.* Quill, 1982.

Igliori, Paola. *Stickman: John Trudell poems, lyrics, talks and conversation.* Inanout Press, New York, 1994.

Indian Country Today, Northern Plains Edition, July 27, 1995.

Indian Country Today, Northern Plains Edition, September 21, 1995.

Jaimes, M. Annette. *The State of Native America, Genocide, Colonization, and Resistance.* South End Press, 1992.

Josephy, Alvin M., Jr. *500 Nations, An Illustrated History of North American Indians.* Alfred A. Knopf, New York, 1994.

—— *The American Heritage Book of Indians.* Bonanza Books. 1982.

Keegan, M.K. *Enduring Culture: A Century of Photography of the Southwest Indians.* Clear

Light Publishers, Santa Fe, NM, 1990.

Kopper, Philip. *The Smithsonian Book of North American Indians; Before the Coming of the Europeans*. Smithsonian Books, Washington, D.C., 1986.

Lester, Joan A. *We're Still Here*. The Children's Museum, Boston, 1987.

Marriott, Alice. *Maria: The Potter of San Ildefonso*. University of Oklahoma Press. 1948.

Means, Russell with Marvin J. Wolf. *Where White Men Fear to Tread*. St. Martin's Press, New York, 1995.

Modern Maturity, Volume 38, Number 5, September-October 1995.

Namias, June, ed. *A Narrative of the Life of Mrs. Mary Jemison by James E. Seaver*. University of Oklahoma Press, 1992.

Native Peoples Magazine: various issues

Ruoff, A. LaVonne Brown. *Indians of North America: Literatures of the American Indian*. Chelsea House Publishers, New York, 1991.

Sandoz, Mari. *These Were the Sioux*. Bison Books, 1985.

Standing Bear, Luther. *Land of the Spotted Eagle*. Bison Books, 1978.

Stuart, Gene S. *America's Ancient Cities*. National Geographic Society, 1988.

Wall, Steve, and Arden, Harvey. *Wisdomkeepers: Meetings with Native American Spiritual Elders*. Beyond Words Publishing, Inc., 1990.

Wall, Steve. *Wisdom's Daughters, Conversations with Women Elders of Native America*. HarperCollins, 1994.

Weatherford, Jack. *Indian Givers: How The Indians of the Americas Transformed the World*. Fawcett Columbine, 1988.

—— *Native Roots: How The Indians Enriched America*. Fawcett Columbine, 1991.

Woodhead, Henry, series ed. *The American Indians Series. The Woman's Way*. Time Life Books, 1995.

ACKNOWLEDGEMENTS

The author would like to thank the following for their contributions and encouragement in the preparation of this book: Rebecca Adamson, President, First Nations Development Institute; Dale Carson; Kate and Libby Hall; Jim Holdsworth, Sr.; Kahn-tineta Horn; Troy Lang; Martha Kate Miller; Trudie Lamb Richmond, Assistant Director, Institute for American Indian Studies; Jeanne Walker Rorex; Delphine Red Shirt, Chairperson, NGO Committee on the International Decade of the World's Indigenous Peoples; staff of the Solidarity Foundation, New York; authors listed in the bibliography; various librarians; the many native people whose thinking and views of life have informed and inspired my own. Any errors in this book are despite the help of those who have contributed generously to its creation. Finally, I wish to thank my husband, Jim Holdsworth, Jr., for his support. The publisher would like to thank Julia Banks Rubel, who edited this book; Emily Head for preparing the index; Gillian Speeth; Cindy Schroeder; and the following individuals and institutions who provided the illustrations:

The Bettmann Archive: Front cover, 2, 10, 13, 21, 25, 27, 35, 37, 54, 56, 59, 68, 75, 90; **The Field Museum, Chicago:** 5 (#13314), 18 (#368), 28 (#A13310), 31 (#33309), 53 (#9511), 63 (#1777), 67 (#2733), 70 (#108394), 74 (#439), 76 (#20676), 83 (#133), 86 (#9468), 87 (#14488); © **Rachel Hunt:** 15 (bottom); **Museum of New Mexico:** 8 (photo by Jesse L. Nusbaum, neg. #61712), 52–3 (photo by T. Harmon Parkhurst, neg. #5144), 72 (neg. #808); **National Archives of Canada:** 39; **Nebraska State Historical Society:** 46; **Peter E. Palmquist Collection:** 20; **Prints and Photographs Division, Library of Congress:** Back cover, 19, 30, 33, 38, 40, 55, 61, 68, 77, 89; Artwork © **Jeanne Walker Rorex:** 7, 93; **South Dakota State Historical Society:** 23 (#DP74.162), 34, 47, 71, 78; **The Southwest Museum, Los Angeles:** 11 (#CT 518 MCC.377), 14 (#CT 518 MCC.288), 92 (#CT 514 MCC.328); © **Michael Tincher:** 15 (top), 81, 84, 85, 88; **UPI/Bettmann Newsphotos:** 26, 43, 44, 45, 49, 50, 69, 79; **Wyoming State Museum—Division of Cultural Resources:** 16, 22 (#19548), 65, 80.

INDEX